D1791262

EL SEGUNDO PUBLIC LIBRARY
3 5156 00273 2211

783.1 BAR
Barbershopping
DISCARDED
c.1

DATE DUE

FEB 1 8 2003		
JUN 2 2 2004		
GAYLORD		PRINTED IN U.S.A.

DISCARDED

Barbershopping

Barbershopping
Musical and Social Harmony

EDITED BY
Max Kaplan

Rutherford • Madison • Teaneck
Fairleigh Dickinson University Press
London and Toronto: Associated University Presses

© 1993 by Associated University Presses, Inc.

All rights reserved. Authorization to photocopy items for internal or personal use, or the internal or personal use of specific clients, is granted by the copyright owner, provided that a base fee of $10.00, plus eight cents per page, per copy is paid directly to the Copyright Clearance Center, 27 Congress Street, Salem, Massachusetts 01970. [0-8386-3504-0/93 $10.00 + 8¢ pp, pc.]

Associated University Presses
440 Forsgate Drive
Cranbury, NJ 08512

Associated University Presses
25 Sicilian Avenue
London WC1A 2QH, England

Associated University Presses
P.O. Box 338, Port Credit
Mississauga, Ontario
Canada L5G 4L8

The paper used in this publication meets the requirements
of the American National Standard for Permanence of Paper
for Printed Library Materials Z39.48-1984.

Library of Congress Cataloging-in-Publication Data

Barbershopping : musical and social harmony / Max Kaplan, editor.
    p. cm.
Includes bibliographical references and index.
ISBN 0-8386-3504-0 (alk. paper)
    1. Barbershop singing—United States. 2. Music and society.
3. Society for the Preservation and Encouragement of Barber Shop Quartet Singing in America. I. Kaplan, Max, 1911– .
ML3516.B37   1993
783.1′422—dc20   91-59053
                                                               CIP
                                                               MN

SECOND PRINTING 1995

PRINTED IN THE UNITED STATES OF AMERICA

Dedicated to

Joe Liles, Executive Director,
SPEBSQSA
Musician, leader, gentleman

Contents

Preface	9
From the Inside—A Descriptive View of SPEBSQSA DEAN ATLEE SNYDER	13
The Respectable Art of Woodshedding in World Music MAX H. BRANDT	33
Becoming a Barbershop Singer ROBERT A. STEBBINS	55
The Leisure Framework PHILLIP BOSSERMAN	73
Barbershoppers and Music Educators: Elitist/Populist Dualisms and the American Music Preservation Problem J. TERRY GATES	95
Barbershoppers as Vestige of the Past and Promise for the Future K. PETER ETZKORN	108
SPEBSQSA's Future: Tradition and Innovation MAX KAPLAN	126
List of Contributors	145
Bibliography	148

Preface

In 1988, on the fiftieth birthday of SPEBSQSA (Society for the Preservation and Encouragement of Barber Shop Quartet Singing in America), Inc., a team of social scientists from the U.S.A. and Canada was created to begin an intensive study of the Society for the Preservation and Encouragement of Barber Shop Quartet Singing in America—more commonly known as Barbershoppers. This remarkable musical hobby or leisure activity has included choruses in its competitions since 1954. Starting informally with a few men in 1938, affiliated groups are to be found now in twenty-eight other countries. Two parallel groups exist for women.

This volume is the result of individual papers by members of the team. Each scholar was invited to go into depth on any issues that pertain to his professional interests. *Dean Snyder,* historian emeritus of SPEBSQSA and a member of many years, was asked to prepare the first paper to identify, in both narrative and interpretative form, the highlights of the Society's half century. The others chose their assignments.

Max Brandt, an avid Barbershopper and professional ethnomusicologist, chose to develop an historical view of "woodshedding."

Robert A. Stebbins of Canada, authority on amateurism, examines the process of becoming a member.

Phillip Bosserman, international authority on leisure, applies this broad concept to barbershopping.

J. Terry Gates, distinguished music educator, examines the concepts of elitist and popular culture as they relate to barbershopping.

K. Peter Etzkorn, eminent sociologist-ethnomusicologist, explores the significance of these thousands of men making "live" music in a "media" world of music.

Finally, the editor-coordinator of the project considers the future of SPEBSQSA within categories of tradition and innovation.

Only on the surface can the barbershoppers—men and women—be simply viewed as persons who enjoy singing and "preserving" a body of songs that was familiar to America in the 1860–

1930 period. Considering the enormity of social, musical, and recreational changes of the past half century, the very existence and persistence of this movement is of sufficient interest to cultural historians or to scholars of leisure and popular culture.

Beyond their personal purpose of enjoyment and the cultural purpose of perpetuation, barbershoppers have served as a significant link from the values of a pre-industrial to those of a postindustrial society. Because of these values, many thousands of men and women from all social and educational backgrounds have been afforded an opportunity to acquire musical skills; they serve their communities; they grow in self-confidence; numerous community groups are amused and enriched by their public appearances; regional and international competitions contribute to aesthetic and performance standards; intangible forms of therapy—consonant with the current perception of "wellness"—may be present as a byproduct of accomplishment and human relationships; finally, this musical-historical hobby has proved capable of providing a concrete human bond among individuals and families in an age of growing impersonalization and media influence.

Whatever value the studies of our small team may have to SPEBSQSA itself—recommendations have not been discouraged—they may serve a long-range purpose of inviting more systematic and penetrating research for social science, adult education, music education, and psychological counselling. Students of family life may profit. As the organization now spreads rapidly to many other parts of the world, ensuing years of observation may even be relevant to world peace.

These studies could not have been undertaken or completed without the complete cooperation of the members and officials of SPEBSQSA, through the international office in Kenosha, Wis. and the many chapters in Canada and the U.S.A. To all of them, symbolized in the able and gentle leadership of Mr. Joe Liles, Executive Director, we extend our deep gratitude.

M. K.

Barbershopping

From the Inside—A Descriptive View of SPEBSQSA

DEAN ATLEE SNYDER

This essay deals with the origins, social foundations, and the organizational history of the "Society for the Preservation and Encouragement of Barber Shop Quartet Singing in America." It does not touch on barbershop harmony per se, although readers should be aware of the stylistic characteristics of such harmony. For a descriptive definition of the Society's musical "product," see the appendix to this chapter. Readers desiring still more information are referred to a technical manual of 400 pages published by SPEBSQSA in 1980 under the title Barbershop Arranging, *or, as a further reference,* Theory of Barbershop Harmony, *also published by the Society.*

Four broad themes will be discussed in this chapter:

I. Time, Place, and Beginning
II. Development and Expansion
III. The Great Awakening
IV. The Society Today

Time, Place, and Beginning

After more than half a century—and to those still living today—life in the decade of the 1930s is a rapidly receding memory. This was the period of the Great Depression, which, in its early years, saw millions unemployed, bread lines and soup kitchens, serious labor unrest, private industry shutdown, bank failures, mortgage foreclosures, and similar misfortune. For many Americans future plans were held in abeyance, pending hoped-for brighter days.

By 1938 the tide was beginning to turn. But Depression-built, government-sponsored, economic and employment relief programs were still relied upon by many families. Everyone recognized such initials as NRA, RFC, WPA, CCC, SSA, HOLC, FDIC, and more. These were the alphabetical agencies of the Federal government—the "New Deal."

For leisure enjoyment, enforced or otherwise, there were radio programs to listen to and movies to attend. There were parks and playgrounds, family picnics, neighborhood parties, amateur sports, and games. For those with dancing feet there were "big bands." There was church on Sunday for the faithful. And with changing times ordinary folk were beginning to sing again because there was something to sing about. True, there were war clouds in Europe but America was at peace.

Out of this increasing mood of optimism came the inspiration of a forty-six-year old lawyer and a group of his friends in Tulsa, Oklahoma. This man was O. C. Cash. He proposed to revive one of the pleasures of his youth—a pastime which required no equipment except the human voice and the love of four-part harmony. With a humorous twinkle in his eye, lawyer Cash and cofounder Rupert Hall, a banker, sought to out-rival the three and four-letter New Deal government agencies by creating a new organization with longer initials—SPEBSQSA. Spelled out it was "The Society for the Preservation and Encouragement of Barber Shop Quartet Singing in America." Later on some referred to this "as the Society with the funny name" and they didn't believe that it existed except as a soon-to-be-forgotten fad or short-lived episode of popular culture.

GETTING STARTED

The new Society held its first meeting in April 1938, attended by twenty-six men "for a song-fest on the Roof Garden of the Tulsa Club." The original intention was only recreation and the fun of singing together as a local group, even though the title suggested a broader scope.

About that time cofounder Cash was quoted as saying, with typical humor for which he was noted, "What this country needs is some good old-fashioned barbershop singing . . . If we're trying to get back to normalcy, let's go all the way back to handlebar mustaches, horsehair sofas, and bicycles built for two."

The idea of a quartet society to revive "the good old songs" had a certain sparkle and humorous quality. The new name was an instant conversation piece. Aided by publicity in the local press, the national wire services, and by several stories in wide circulation magazines, inquiries came to Cash and his local group almost immediately asking, "How can I join?" Cash replied by sending membership cards at his own expense and deputizing those who inquired about joining to form local chapters similar to the one in Tulsa.

The seed of quartet singing as recreation soon took root and sprouted in other places. First were Kansas City and St. Louis where Cash had business friends; then in Hollywood, where Bing Crosby mentioned the new Society in one of his radio programs. Next were Chicago, Detroit, Cleveland, and Pittsburgh; and eventually east to the Atlantic seaboard, sparked by Mayor LaGuardia's plan to have an invitational quartet contest at the New York World's Fair in 1940.

The new Society did not have any set plan of organization at first. But as momentum increased, Cash took out formal incorporation papers in late 1938 as a legal entity in order to protect its name.

Early membership statistics are fragmentary. By 1941–42 perhaps 2,000 membership cards had been issued for the fifty-five local chapters. The Society is now more than fifty years old. In one recent year its membership reached a peak of 38,000 in the U.S. and Canada, with several thousands more in overseas affiliates. The passing years have brought other changes which await description.

However, the character of the organization itself first needs attention before tracing further organizational development.

TYPICALLY AMERICAN

The habit and custom of banding together in groups for a common purpose is typically American. The French observer, Alexis de Tocqueville, was astounded by the number and variety of our civic societies. He wrote, "In no country in the world has the principle of association been more successfully applied to a greater multitude of objects than in America . . . There is no end . . . to the combined powers of individuals combined in a society." The Society for the Preservation and Encouragement of Barber Shop Quartet Singing in America fulfills this early prediction.

WHO ARE WE

Although holding fast to the barbershop style in its harmony singing, the Society has changed and broadened its purposes and program over the years. Some members have felt that these changes have been too great and that the Society has lost the casual, free-wheeling, sheer fun-loving, recreational hobby aspects with which it began.

Today we are a voluntary association in the best American tradition. A man can join, or not join; remain a member or drop out; accept administrative responsibility or "let George do IT;" participate in singing casually or intensively. In many chapters, if age impairments or job pressures interfere, he can be a "listening member" without the requirements of singing participation. The privilege of membership is an open door to many and varied kinds of growth, development, and leisure-time enjoyment. Some years ago a keynote speaker called the Society "Many hobbies within a hobby—musical, social, recreational, and educational."

It may further be said that SPEBSQSA is not promoting a "cause," an economic idea, a charitable service, or any similar example of group action. The Society's primary aim is to create and enjoy a "product." And that product (our music), however intangible it may seem, requires specialized individual and ensemble effort and increased excellence of "production." We constantly exhibit our product to ourselves as members, and to those outside our organization—that is, the general public.

A GUILD OF FINE ARTS

The craft of barbershop music is an art form wherein we are constantly creating and recreating an artistic product. Our members are practitioners of the art form and, as such, our Society may be compared to the concept of a "guild" as it was known in medieval times.

Guilds were societies of artisans (stone masons, silversmiths, wood carvers, etc.). Their members were skilled in production and enormously proud of their specialized product. Based on this concept, one of our early and greatly admired SPEBSQSA chapters in the 1940s described and advertised itself as "A guild of quartet singers."

As craftsmen, we seek to produce and display a worthy product. But our vision, our aim, requires a broader statement. Here is how we describe ourselves today:

> The Society is to be a widely recognized, evergrowing, singing fraternity of men, drawn together by their love of the four-part, a cappella, close harmony style of music known as Barbershop, whose mission is

to perpetuate that style by sharing it and their love for it with people of all ages throughout the world.

Development and Expansion

We return now to our earliest days as a Society in order to see what actually took place. It was a slow process of arriving at an organizational structure, finding leadership, developing a contest and judging procedure, and eventually a substructure of intermediate districts between the national (later international) entity and the local chapters. Early on the Society adopted a system of quartet (and later chorus) competition which soon became a driving force.

The framework and governance of SPEBSQSA was not preordained by formal design. Growth came in piecemeal fashion by a slow process of accretion—as a river changes its channel or builds up a delta at the river's mouth. O. C. Cash and Rupert Hall had a pregnant idea which was followed by several years of slow gestation for an embryonic Society.

At first there was no formal Board of Directors, although early letterheads listed some well-recognized national celebrities, among whom were Sam Breedon, owner of the St. Louis Cardinals baseball team, Governor Ralph Carr of Colorado, Bing Crosby of Hollywood, Sigmund Spaeth, music historian and radio personality, Pat O'Brien, movie actor, and others of like status. So far as is known, none of them ever attended a business or organizational meeting.

Correspondence piled up and newspaper clippings came from far and wide that first year, 1938–39. *Time* magazine said "No mere anything-for-a-laugh letterhead organization, SPEBSQSA takes itself fairly seriously." The *Reader's Digest* wrote "Celebrities and unknowns, rich men and poor, have been drawn together in one of the most democratic organizations America has ever had." Such publicity was nourishing food for an infant idea.

Finally, word went out that in June 1939 a "World's Championship Quartet Contest" would be held in Tulsa. No one knew how many would come. A total of 150 men came from seven States and seventeen cities. A short business meeting was held to elect a national president and other officers, but no formal minutes were written. But there was a quartet contest and a winner was picked. The thrill of competition was added to the sheer joy of informal quartet singing in the barbershop style which had been the original concept.

The second annual meeting and quartet contest was held at the New York World's Fair in 1940. There were thirty-two quartets in competition, geographically spread west to Wichita and Oklahoma City, south to Jacksonville and Miami, and north to Boston. The largest group of delegates, thirty-five, came from St. Louis in a chartered railway car. They had the votes to capture the third annual convention and quartet contest for St. Louis the following summer of 1941.

The newly appointed Board of Directors met in January 1941 to plan the next convention. The fledgling organization had scant financial resources naturally, but agreed on a draft constitution. This was the beginning of the society's formal system of governance.

The new constitution was written by Carroll Adams of Detroit, who soon became national president and later (after Canada joined the Society in 1944) international executive secretary. He, our first paid officer, served in that capacity until 1953.

A REMARKABLE PERIOD OF LEADERSHIP AND GROWTH

The next ten years, including the war years, 1941–45, produced a tremendous growth in membership and local chapters—a record which today is amazing to recall. In 1942 the Society had about 2,000 members; by 1950 nearly 27,000. The number of chapters increased from fifty-five to more than 600, including those in Canada. In 1952, despite a downswing, there were more than 24,000 members.

These statistics are overshadowed by a most remarkable combination of officers and board members who had been selected to guide the Society's affairs. They were a self-perpetuating group, attracted to the Society by their love of barbershop harmony and earlier memories of quartet singing in that style. They were not celebrities, but successful men of business and professional experience, well able to finance their hobby participation. Men like Staab, Embury, Martin, Thorne, Reagan, the Merrill brothers, Cole, Diekema, Boardman, and a small cadre of others like them, will be long remembered in this capacity. They were generous with their time as volunteers and craftsmen in both our music and our administration.

The Society's paid staff was minimal during this period. In his first several years secretary Adams had only one clerical assistant.

From the Inside—A Descriptive View of SPEBSQSA

By 1952, with more than 24,000 members, the staff numbered only a dozen employees. The real work of the Society was done by volunteers—individually and through committees. When Frank Thorne was international president in 1947 he mobilized twenty volunteer committees on Society projects. International board meetings twice a year were strenuous work sessions lasting several days with vigorous debate on controversial issues, and with each member paying his own expenses to attend. It was not unusual for a board agenda to contain forty or more separate items for information and discussion.

Early leaders were ardent organizers of new chapters in their respective states and metropolitan areas. For example, international president Cole personally organized eight chapters in Wisconsin. Carroll Adams was well known in Michigan for his work with the Board of Trade and the Michigan Alumni Association and he organized or assisted in chapter formation in many places. So did Hal Staab when he traveled through New England on business. Enthusiasm was high in widely scattered towns and cities for spreading this new and exciting hobby.

COMPETITIVE SINGING AS A DRIVING FORCE

The early development of a system of contest judging received much attention. For the first several years there was no accepted standard of adjudication. Judging was informal. A judge might take notes on the back of an envelope for later backstage discussion with his colleagues. The need for separate scoring categories for example, harmony accuracy or stage presence, was recognized later. By 1944 there were preprinted score sheets and a separate judge or judges for each category. In 1946 judge-training sessions were first held, and in 1949 rather stringent judge-certification procedures were adopted. It soon became well accepted doctrine "that healthy competition affords the best means of perfecting the art of barbershop quartet singing." This same doctrine was applied later to competitive chorus singing. Those members who would have preferred a noncompetitive philosophy (including a significant group of early leaders) were soon overcome by the substantial majority view.

MUSICAL ACCLAIM—OR THE LACK OF IT

Beginning in 1941, the Society published a quarterly (later bi-monthly) magazine distributed to all members. Instructional articles on musical subjects were included from time to time. An early title was "The Mechanics of Barbershop Chord Relationships." At annual and mid-winter Society meetings in the late 1940s there was some attempt to develop specialized training and instruction in judging, song leading, and quartet coaching, but not for the membership at large. Those members who could read music had reference to printed, Society-approved, song arrangements. However, for many men singing in the barbershop style their effort was based on repetitious rote-learning or ear-singing of four-part chords which seemed to harmonize well, but they didn't know why. The average members technical music knowledge was usually quite sketchy.

All this is not to say that the best (the competitive) quartet members did not engage in rigorous practice sessions or develop self-improvement techniques, but only that singing together for the general membership at chapter meetings was in the mode of a casual, catch-as-catch-can experience. However, to all concerned the result was always pleasing and fun-loving recreation.

The foregoing may explain why, in an earlier period of Society history many, perhaps most, professionally trained musicians held the barbershop style of singing in low esteem. The *Harvard Dictionary of Music,* for example, called the style "banal" and "oversweet." In defense the Society and its leadership may well have had an institutional inferiority complex. To them it was just a hobby that was not too well understood or accepted by outside observers.

And yet there were notable exceptions. Some music educators joined the Society and liked what they saw and heard. A book on choral arranging, written by a leading professor at Columbia University, contained a chapter on the four-part barbershop style. For two consecutive years in the late 1940s the District of Columbia chapter sang in joint concert in Constitution Hall with the National Symphony Orchestra. It was a sell-out audience both times for a mixture of light orchestral classics interspersed with barbershop ballads and upbeat tunes. The shows closed with the orchestra and chorus performing a Barbershop Medley specially arranged for the occasion and patterned after the Boston Pops program style.

Generally speaking, however, in its early years SPEBSQSA tended to build an organizational fence around its activities and to remain aloof from national music organizations, local choral groups and performing arts councils. With the passage of time, these barriers fortunately began to break down in favor of genuine cooperative effort.

ARMED FORCES COLLABORATION

The Society did reach out beyond its self-imposed boundaries in one area. In the late 1940s the military services decided to encourage barbershop singing as an off-duty recreational activity for soldiers, airmen, and naval personnel. The Society was asked to help. Monthly BSQ quartet arrangements were included in each issue of the "Army Hit Kit" of popular songs which went to military units of all services. Simple training manuals were prepared. Local contests were held, aided by local chapters of the Society. SPEBSQSA champion quartets toured military bases and went overseas to entertain and instruct troops in the barbershop style. In 1952 a military quartet from the armed forces, "The Four Teens," won the Society's international quartet championship. Its members were all under the age of twenty-one years.

A PERIOD OF UNCERTAINTY AND CONCERN

Having expanded into Canada in 1944, the Society reached a peak of growth in 1950 with a membership of 26,900 in 661 chapters. A marked decline in size then began—down to 22,600 in 1954. This was a loss of 4,300 members in four years. It was an unexpected and baffling change of circumstance. Society leaders were deeply disturbed.

What was the reason for the decline? The signals were first noticed at the midwinter meeting of the international board at Toronto in 1952. Soon thereafter board members were asked for written comments. There were no clear answers. Local leadership had fallen away, some said. Perhaps the fad of Barbershop singing—like all fads—had a life cycle of its own. Was the clock winding down? The country was then involved in the Korean War. Was that a factor? One board member wrote: "Chapters are loath to interest themselves in civic affairs and activities that would build local prestige." And so it went.

There was such concern that a blue-ribbon, select group of twelve prominent members, including founder Cash, was appointed and charged with a long-range planning function. For the first time the Society sought to do an in-depty study of its strengths and weaknesses. In a keynote speech to the Society's

House of Delegates (June 1953) the chairman of this committee said:

> We have begun to examine our growth in qualitative rather than quantitative terms. We are a quartet society, yes, but a lot more than that. There are many opportunities for personal, musical and social growth. Our program can have many dimensions ... SPEBSQSA is based on music and our style of arranging 4-part a cappella harmony for male voices can produce good music. But we are not sufficiently well understood by those who often control or influence the community's attitude toward music. We must reach out beyond our present boundaries for greater influence and status.

The Great Awakening

The long-range planning committee's final report, titled "Twenty Proposals," charted a new path for the Society. SPEBSQSA changed its focus gradually. It was on the way to becoming a different organization. The hobby aspects were still there. But now there was more.

There were at least four factors which changed the character of the Society in the 1950s. These may be identified for further discussion as: (1) Acceptance of the planning process and its goals; (2) Acceptance of competitive choral singing; (3) Acceptance of family orientation; and (4) Acceptance of barbershop craft training for all members.

PLANNING PROCESS AND RECOMMENDATIONS

Among the twenty proposals accepted for action by the international board of directors in 1954 were these: (1) Enlarge the Society's purpose (which heretofore was simply "To perpetuate the barbershop quartet ... and encourage good fellowship"); (2) Give training in music and barbershop craft to every member; (3) Elevate chorus singing to greater prominence; (4) Embark without delay on a program of chapter leadership training; (5) Develop closer relations with local music teachers and choral groups and with allied groups in the arts and recreation and (6) Publish a professionally written text to explain and illustrate the barbershop style and choral arrangements in that style. (The above items are condensed and paraphrased from the full report and do not include other items which addressed the internal management and membership problems in the Society as it then existed.)

Another important step was taken two years later by action of the Internal Revenue Service. The Society, until then merely designated as a nonprofit fraternal association, was now recognized for tax purposes as a "Charitable, literary and educational organization." For SPEBSQSA the key word here soon became member "education," or the study of barbershop craft as it was called.

The Society's long-range planning committee was paralleled quickly by similar committees at the district level and by many chapters. Goals were established and new program enthusiasm became evident. A membership upturn soon appeared. The Society was awake with new life and vigor. But long-range planning and changes in legal status did not tell the whole story of what has been called "the great awakening." There were other aspects.

GROUP HARMONIZING—INFORMAL STYLE

What started out as emphasis on quartet activity had from earliest days the added emphasis of "gang singing," as it was termed. At chapter meetings the entire group would join in harmonizing familiar songs. The leader was a member who had a memory for words and tunes and the enthusiasm to say "Let's sing." Sometimes he was a music teacher or choir director—oftentimes not. He made no attempt to polish the interpretation of a song or balance the voice parts—only to keep the group together in harmony. "Woodshed harmony" it was called. When one song ended another began. A member who was unfamiliar with a song could sing "off the ear" of his neighbor, harmonizing his voice part as best he could. Printed music was rarely, if ever, used, but song sheets or booklets containing words only were frequently available.*

At barbershop "parades" or concerts, and at contests to which the public was invited, the entire audience would join in this type of music-making. It was called a sing-along or "community singing." In the mid-1940s some attempt was made to identify and train Society members as "community song leaders." When an

---

*See the essay by Max Brandt in this volume.

audience of several thousand people joined voices in this way, it was thrilling to hear the group harmonies produced.

GROUP HARMONIZING—THE ORGANIZED CHORUS

Chorus singing was different. In the 1940s some SPEBSQSA chapters of large size had a smaller unit called the chapter chorus. These men often met separately to learn and polish to greater perfection their barbershop repertoire. Other chapters regarded the entire membership as their chapter chorus and sought out skilled musical leadership to direct the ensemble effort. Printed music was always used for rehearsal until the chorus had memorized the song and its vocal interpretation.

Some districts of the Society began to sponsor chorus competition among their chapters and to select winners. Taking notice of this, the Society issued its first reference material on choral training in 1948. The first folio of arrangements specifically for choral use, *Songs for the Chorus,* was issued in 1951. The same year (June 1951) came the first choral director's workshop as a program feature of the Toledo international convention. There were forty-four chorus directors present.

COMPETITIVE CHORAL SINGING

Further organized chorus competition resulted from an experimental contest at the Detroit convention in 1953 to see if there was general acceptance of the competitive concept. This was followed by a fully structured international contest at the 1954 Washington convention with each district represented in competition. There has been an annual contest since then to select an international winner. A chorus representing Great Britain was added to the list of participants in 1990, and in 1991 a chorus of young men from Sweden competed. It is expected that choruses from other overseas affiliates will be competitors eventually.

The emergence of competitive choral singing gave an added stimulus to the Society's new program of music education and training. It provided an opportunity for participation and recognition to many members who did not sing (or care to sing) in organized quartets. It relied upon chorus directors (professionally trained or not) willing to use their choral leadership and teaching skills. Today each chapter's table of organization includes a vice president for music, the chorus director, assistant director(s), section leaders, librarian, and chorus manager—all referred to as "The Music Team."

All this developed from small beginnings as part of the Society's "great awakening." Chorus singing and quartet singing have thus gained equal prominence both in their hobby aspects and in the opportunity for making better music and better public presentation.

A FAMILY ORIENTED ORGANIZATION EMERGES

An early Society legend says that founder Cash once quipped, "I have no objection to women attending our contests, but I do think they should be kept under strict control at all times." Knowing the Cash brand of humor, it is certain that this was said with only mock-serious intent, for Cash was a devoted family man. But it is true that for a considerable time the Society's posture was strictly male.

One outgrowth of the increased choral emphasis noted above was to greatly enlarge attendance at Society conventions and interchapter gatherings. Wives and children began to accompany their husbands and fathers to their events in support of their quartet and chorus endeavors.

Sensing this trend, convention planners arranged special activities for family members. Children, called "Barber-teens," received special attention. A ladies luncheon was always scheduled and there was a special hospitality room set aside for them. For many members conventions became an opportunity for a family vacation. Post-convention tours to historic places were added. Whereas in the 1940s Society events attracted almost exclusively the male species, the 1950s and later decades brought much larger attendance including family members and friends—reaching at times as many as 10,000 at the annual summer conventions.

Another SPEBSQSA development involving the family came at the chapter level. It soon became the custom for most local chapters to encourage the formation of a women's (non-singing) auxiliary, meeting socially as a group, attending contests as a cheering section for their quartets and chorus, and assisting in chapter money-raising and charitable projects.

Family orientation is firmly established today. It further identifies a changed role for the Society—from a purely male hobby organization to one of greater scope and social affinity. It is part of the great awakening which began in the 1950s.

THE STUDY OF BARBERSHOP CRAFT

The most pronounced awakening or changeover in the history of SPEBSQSA came with the introduction of training in barbershop craft. The history of all sports and hobbies leads inevitably to an emphasis on technique and training. Some participants are naturally more adept than others. Some participants learn by trial and error, while others observe and copy the best features of what they see, hear, and do. Eventually the level of performance is upgraded. A record is made of what works and what doesn't. Those who have skill and knowledge demonstrate it to others. Those who are articulate compile, discuss, write, and teach. Those who are inventive and innovative propose and test new schemes and methods and publicize the results. This is the road we have travelled in SPEBSQSA in developing barbershop craft.

In 1948 came a new idea—the quartet clinic. It originated in the District of Columbia chapter which, at that time, boasted nineteen organized quartet groups singing regularly. A championship quartet from another city was imported to share their expertise and to observe and critique actual performances by chapter quartets. The idea was expanded at the 1950 midwinter convention with one clinic about rehearsal techniques and another to test judge candidates for judging positions.

A NEW TERMINOLOGY

The first known use of the term "barbershop craft" came in January 1952. A music educator, Dr. Harold Arberg, was chorus director of the Alexandria, Virginia, chapter. Most of its members, although enthusiastic singers, were musically untrained. Dr. Arberg proposed a thirty-minute series of teaching and training sessions in music fundamentals to be part of each chapter meeting extending over a ten-week period. Topics included key signatures, note values, scales, clefs, chord structure, and characteristics of the barbershop style of chord use and voicing, as contrasted with the glee-club style. Exercises in sight reading were included. The teaching method was elementary. Simple illustrative devices were used, such as the blackboard and the piano. Some melodies not well adapted to the barbershop style were demonstrated.

The Alexandria chapter responded favorably. Word of this development soon spread and Dr. Arberg was invited to present his ideas, which he called barbershop craft, to other nearby chapters and to Society leaders at the district and international levels. An international barbershop craft committee was appointed to spearhead the effort, and a section of each issue of the Society's magazine was devoted to the subject. All chapters were encouraged to include craft sessions as a regular program feature, adapted to the experience level of their general membership.

As time went on craft instruction came to have a broader focus including, for example, script-writing, show production, audio techniques, and the role of the master of ceremonies. The effort was not only to improve the individual member's understanding of, and excellence in, musicianship, but also to improve the Society's "product" in better public presentation of music in the barbershop style.

HARMONY COLLEGE

A giant leap forward came in August 1961 on a Minnesota college campus. For four days of intensive training 400 men, coming from thirty-seven states and six Canadian provinces, studied barbershop craft in its several aspects. Classes were held from 8:A.M. to 12:00 P.M. and included basic harmony and music fundamentals, quartet promotion and coaching, chorus development, song arranging in the barbershop style, script writing, and stagecraft. There was much informal music-making between class sessions, and on the final night a quartet and chorus concert in the college auditorium.

For the next several years similar summer schools devoted to harmony education programs (HEP) were held on five college campuses, chosen coast-to-coast to give more members easier travel access.

For more than twenty years, the HEP schools, now called Harmony College, have been full seven-day sessions held at a centrally located university campus in Missouri. Enrollment is limited to 700 students. Students can select from more than fifty week-long courses. The faculty consists of experienced, professionally trained men, drawn from the Society as well as from outside sources and educational institutions.

The Society's most recent adventure in teaching and training, known as the Directors College, held its first week-long session in June 1990 on the Carthage College campus in Kenosha, Wisconsin. Attendance was limited to established chorus directors plus others with musical background who might want to become a director. A total of 345 men attended from the United States and six Canadian provinces, with eight chapter chorus directors coming from Great Britain.

The SPEBSQSA education and training program includes much more. Each of the Society's sixteen districts has an annual three-day miniature Harmony College. Music leadership is also covered as a separate subject at each district's annual Chapter Officers Training School (COTS). Most chapters have frequent craft sessions for member improvement. On its international staff, headquartered in Kenosha, the Society has a team of nine experienced and professionally credentialed "music men" available to develop new arrangements and folios, produce craft manuals and other instructional aids (including audio-visual materials), and to serve as instructors at the colleges and schools mentioned above. These men have pioneered an impressive array of teaching materials and methods not generally available except to Society members and their overseas affiliate groups. Each district of the Society has an appointed unpaid volunteer music educator to assist the headquarters staff men. Chapter musical leadership is strengthened constantly because of all this.

Barbershop craft, which started in a small way in 1952 to develop greater knowledge and proficiency among Society members, and better public presentation of the barbershop style, has blossomed to become one of the finest adult education programs to be found anywhere in the fields of music and recreation.

THE CHALLENGE OF PLURALISM

Since the great awakening, two notable differences of opinion continue to be heard in friendly, yet healthy, opposition. The first is voiced by those members who prefer to sing in the barbershop style merely for their own private pleasure and for occasional public entertainment. On the other side are those who derive pleasure from the contest system and are willing to spend many hours in regimented rehearsal to win competitive rewards for their quartet or chorus. Men of both persuasions are found in the average chapter. Some quartets sing only for fun, others are contest-minded. Some chapter choruses (especially those of large size) find competition to be a primary goal. Some neighboring chapters, however, may compete only occasionally while some are totally non-competitive.

A second field of debate is a variation of the first. In recent years a vigorous minority has argued that the present-day Society has forgotten its roots which were solely those of quartet singing. Their position is that organized chorus singing (especially of the competitive variety) has taken over the front stage in too many chapters, with the result that quartet singing has accepted a secondary role, and in some chapters has virtually disappeared. The best chapters, of course, give equal emphasis both to their quartets and their chorus. One prominent chapter of international chorus championship fame, has more than twenty registered quartets singing regularly and many more informal foursomes on a "put-together" basis.

The answer to these two fields of argument is for the Society to accept the philosophy of pluralism, and to provide better balance and wider options in chapter programs. Chapter goals should provide such flexibility. This is now being done on an ever-widening basis. In addition, quartet formation and coaching is being stressed at all SPEBSQSA Harmony Colleges. The concept of noncompetitive choral festivals is also being considered. Several spin-off groups of Society members have been meeting annually to engage in non-competitive quartet singing, and to keep alive the art of woodshedding, which is strictly harmonizing and chord-structuring by ear rather than by adaptation to printed music. These positive steps are being well received by the membership, while recognizing that in an organization such as ours a single answer is never the complete answer.

A senior Society historian wrote recently in the Society's magazine:

> Despite these past debates, we have maintained a remarkable spirit of unity amidst diversity . . . Can we now recognize that pluralism is one of the lessons of our history? Hopefully, yes!

The Society Today

The decade of the 1990s is here. The Society known as SPEBSQSA is now more than fifty years old. It is no longer merely a hobby organization. It is no longer merely a quartet society, although that activity remains a central focus and thousands of quartet groups are singing together regularly, both for their own recreational enjoyment and in public performance.

With few exceptions, every local chapter now sings together as an organized chorus and with frequent opportunities in the local community to entertain the public, perhaps substitute for a church choir during summer vacation, or to sing the national anthem at an athletic or patriotic event. The typical chorus repertoire contains tuneful popular melodies, patriotic and sacred numbers, and songs from the musical stage—always with emphasis on those songs which will adapt to the barbershop style.

In the more than 800 towns and cities where chapters exist, the Society finds cultural allies through membership in community arts councils and in working with other musical organizations, including women's groups which also sing in the barbershop style.

Chapters are urged to volunteer in support of local civic and charitable activities and music scholarship programs, and the official voice of the Society is heard in favor of maintaining strong public school programs of music and the performing arts.

Using the theme "We sing that they shall speak," the Society raises a large sum each year to help support the Institute of Logopedics in its programs of research and treatment for children with speech impairments, especially where music can be used as an adjunct to therapy.

At its international headquarters the Society maintains a music-publishing activity and the largest reference collection of popular sheet music outside the Library of Congress in Washington. Also at headquarters is an attractively presented museum reflecting the development of the barbershop style and the early history of the Society. A professional curator supervises the museum and is available to assist college and university students desiring to do research using the Society's historical collections.

The Society has affiliate relationships with the Music Educators National Conference (MENC) and the American Choral Directors Association (ACDA), and its best quartets and choruses frequently appar on the convention programs of these organizations. Units of the Society have appeared in joint concert with the Mormon Tabernacle Choir in Salt Lake City, and in gala concerts at both the Kennedy Center and the Wolf Trap Performing Arts Center in Washington, D.C. There have also been appearances at the White House and the Supreme Court in Washington, at Lake Chautauqua in western New York State, on the concert stage at Carnegie Hall in New York City, and with a number of local symphony orchestras.

The Society has chapters in every state and Canadian province. Its total membership has stabilized at about 37,000, with some variation yearly. The median age of the membership edges upward in line with general population trends. Fathers and sons, and even grandsons, often sing together in the same chapter and champion quartets often have members in their early twenties.

The Society aspires to attract men from all segments of the age spectrum who love to sing and who enjoy good recreational fellowship. Increase in the numerical size of membership continues to be important, exceeded only by emphasis on quality and the continued outreach of the Society's substantive programs.

On a worldwide basis the Society has formal affiliation agreements with groups singing in the barbershop style in Great Britain, Sweden, Holland, Germany, Australia, New Zealand, and South Africa. Nonaffiliated groups are known in many other overseas locations including Ireland, Singapore, Israel, Saudi Arabia, Austria, Spain, American Samoa, and the former Soviet Union, whose quartet, The Quiet Don, toured America in 1990.

A World Harmony Council, with broad representation from overseas affiliates, has been created and is being financed by SPEBSQSA. Its purpose is to encourage and facilitate relationships wherever barbershop harmony is being sung. Publications and expertise in barbershop craft are being shared on a broad basis by the Society's professional music staff. Travel groups representing chapters of the Society in the U.S. and Canada frequently go abroad on vacation tours, combining barbershop concerts and quartet appearances with the pleasures of sightseeing. Reciprocal visits bring foreign barbershoppers to our shores. It is expected that by the year 2000 one of the annual SPEBSQSA conventions, or an International Music Festival, will be scheduled to meet in London, England. Looking ahead to increased worldwide expansion, the Society's board of directors has rephrased its former motto, "Keep America Singing," to "Keep the Whole World Singing."

A FINAL WORD

With pride in its history, and with a desire to fulfill its accepted musical and educational role and to be a respected recreational asset locally, nationally and internationally, the Society for the Preservation and Encouragement of Barber Shop Singing [sic] (quartets and choruses alike) looks to the future with confidence.

Appendix

FROM THE SPEBSQSA CONTEST & JUDGING HANDBOOK

Definition of Barbershop Harmony

Barbershop Harmony is a style of unaccompanied vocal music characterized by consonant four part chords for every melody note. Occasional brief passages may be sung by fewer than four voice parts.

The voice parts are called Tenor, Lead, Baritone and Bass. The melody is consistently sung by the Lead, with the Tenor harmonizing above the melody, the Bass singing the lowest harmonizing notes below the melody, and the Baritone completing the chord either above or below the melody. The melody may be sung occasionally by the Bass, but not by the Tenor except for an infrequent note or two to avoid awkward voice leading, and in introductions or tags (codas).

Barbershop music features major and minor chords and barbershop (dominant-type) seventh chords, resolving primarily on the circle of fifths. Sixth, ninth, and major seventh chords are avoided except where demanded by the melody, while chords containing the minor second interval are not used. The basic harmonization may be embellished with additional chord progressions to provide harmonic interest and rhythmic momentum, to carry over between phrases, or to introduce or close the song effectively.

Barbershop interpretive style permits relatively wide liberties in the treatment of note values—staying within proper musical form—and uses changes in tempo and volume to more effectively create a mood and tell a story artistically.

Relative to an established sense of tonality, the melody line and the harmony parts are enharmonically adjusted in pitch to produce an optimum consonant sound. The resulting pitch relationships are often considerably at variance with those defined by the equal temperament of fixed pitch instruments. Use of similar word sounds in good quality and optimum volume relationships by each of the voice parts further enhances the sensation of consonance by mutual reinforcement of the harmonics (overtones) to produce the unique full or "expanded" sound characteristic of barbershop harmony.

The Respectable Art of Woodshedding in World Music

MAX H. BRANDT

One of the interesting discussions taking place in barbershop quartet circles today focuses on the dichotomy between ear singing and note singing, between fixed harmonic arrangements of songs in the barbershop style, as opposed to improvised renditions of the same. Harmonizing among barbershoppers once implied spontaneous harmony without the aid of written notes, and the method was mainstream. Today this rare form of harmonic improvisation is better known as "woodshedding" among members of the Society for the Preservation and Encouragement of Barbershop Quartet Singing in America, Inc., hereinafter referred to as the "Society."

This debate is not as vociferous as others, such as the heated controversy over quartet versus chorus prominence, or the pros and cons of contests, and what is and isn't barbershop in melody and harmony. In fact, in the eyes of many of today's barbershoppers, woodshedding is simply a lost cause, an outmoded form of entertainment that is not worthy of serious concern. Nevertheless, there is a growing number of people in the Society who maintain that woodshedding is indeed a subject of major importance, and one that calls for continued reflection among devoted barbershoppers. Like disputes among the followers of any art form, it reflects the pressures of historic and social change. The subject is especially germane to those individuals, generally age fifty and above, who learned the art of woodshedding informally, under the lamppost and in the barbershop, well before they ever thought about joining the ranks of an organization that was formed to preserve and encourage this art form. These are the people who believe that woodshedding is not only a joyful exercise, but also an important creative art form, and one that should command much more respect than it presently receives.

The term woodshedding means different things to different

people. The woodshed was once the place in this country where a boy was paddled or "worked over" by his father for being naughty. That rustic place for storing and preparing firewood is no longer known to most North Americans, but from it we have inherited a verb that generally means "working something over," in the sense of preparing or improving something, and in the musical context is akin to rehearsing.

Among barbershoppers today the term woodshedding has a more particular connotation, referring to any spontaneous harmonizing without the aid of a prescribed arrangement, often by a spontaneous "pick-up" quartet, composed of four people who do not normally sing together. It is not unlike a group of jazz musicians who, meeting each other for the first time, take out their instruments to do a little informal jamming, not necessarily for public consumption, but for fun among themselves.

In the early days of the Society, though, and before it was organized, woodshedding had a somewhat different connotation, referring more to the process of refining an oral arrangement of a particular song, perhaps in anticipation of a public performance. The current practice of rehearsing a Society arrangement over a period of time could be considered woodshedding by the standard definition of the term, but to today's barbershoppers that term generally refers to spontaneous harmonic improvisation, without the help of prescribed arrangements. It is a practice that now generally takes place, if at all, after the Society chorus rehearsal—at the "afterglow." It is extremely rare today to find a Society quartet performing in public a piece that has been learned through the old woodshedding method; such behavior would be considered substandard by most members of the Society.

My own introduction to barbershopping was pure woodshedding, in a small New England town during the 1940s, before the age of ten. The performers were men who neither sang from written arrangements nor belonged to the Society. One of them, my dad, would invite fellow harmonizers to the house, usually on a weekend afternoon or evening, to share a little moonshine, friendship, and surprisingly beautiful harmony. (On second thought, woodshedding sessions often got underway before high noon!). These were not well educated bards, nor could any of them read music, but they certainly were masters of melody and harmony.

Such were the early music lessons of most of today's ardent woodshedders. They did lots of listening and imitating, and were eventually invited to join tne fray. Many of us underestimate early childhood exposure to music in the development of appreciation and performance; just as language learning comes most naturally during the preschool years, so does music. Many seasoned woodshedders had this kind of musical upbringing, listening to vocal groups on the radio, harmonizing with relatives at home, with the congregation at church, or with friends in any number of informal settings. Social life in the United States before the days of television nurtured this kind of self-entertainment.

In contrast, a growing number of today's barbershoppers, especially those young enough to be reared in the age of television and a very different brand of popular music, were brought into the fold in a much more formal manner: through chapter meetings of the Society, well after their youthful formative years of musical learning. I have heard one or two of the old timers speak of this latter form of instruction in the art of barbershopping as artificial insemination, which was not necessarily meant to be a compliment. Such skeptics, though, are also usually quick to recognize that without the Society to bring singers together, there wouldn't be much harmony left in the woodshed.

To Woodshed or not to Woodshed

As mentioned earlier, woodshedding is currently looked upon with a touch of disdain by a good number of well-meaning members of the Society who may value woodshedding as an important historical link to a rustic past, but still distance themselves, for the sake of progress, from this "inferior" form of singing. To the contrary, earnest ear singers view woodshedding as the pinnacle of the art form, the height of achievement, the frosting on the cake. This latter category of singers includes not only street corner riffraff who never learned to read notes, but also musically literate and celebrated members of the Society who appreciate the exhilaration of singing a well-written Society arrangement with a good quartet. Fortunately, such literate barbershoppers can still savor the delight of creating harmonies extemporaneously, which can be equally pleasurable but somehow different, maybe more inspirational, than ringing the chords of an urbane written arrangement.

We can learn more about this dichotomy by pondering a standard encyclopedia definition of a barbershop quartet, author unnamed:

BARBERSHOP QUARTET, form of informal choral music performed in the United States, consisting of improvising harmonies to popular melodies. The phrase either dates from an era when barbershops formed social and musical centers for a neighborhood's males or refers back to the British expression 'barber's music,' meaning extemporized performance by patrons waiting to be shaved and referring to barbers' traditional roles as musicians. (Encyclopedia Britannica 1978)

If the author of this definition were to rewrite it today, based upon visits to any number of Society chapters around the United States, the wording of the first sentence would probably change from "informal" to "formal," reflecting current performance style, and "improvising" would be substituted by the word "arranged."

It is worth contemplating the importance of harmonic improvisation in the barbershop style in the decades prior to 1938 when the Society was formed. How intriguing it would be to journey back to several locations in the United States on a given night, let's say in June of 1910, 1920, or maybe 1930, to sample a wide variety of barbershop quartet performances. One could observe the genre from a number of different perspectives—repertory, ethnic background of performers, sound quality, costume of the day, occasion for the performance—to name a few. We might be able to determine how much of the harmony would be based on a prescribed arrangement, and how much would result from harmonic improvisations in the oral tradition. We would expect most of the performances to be improvised, with only a few following prescribed arrangements.

The flourishing years of barbershop harmony began in the mid-1890s and started to decline noticeably by the mid-1930s, with the golden age of this era falling somewhere between the turn of the century and the roaring twenties. We also know that some of the well-known quartets of the period sang from written arrangements, sometimes put to script by a member of the quartet or a local musician. In fact, some of the barbershop favorites from Tin Pan Alley were published with four-part arrangements, usually of the refrain but not the verses, on the back page of the song sheet. Therefore, the purpose here is not to dispute the fact that the quartets of the golden age occasionally sang from printed or hand-written arrangements; perhaps the best of them did. Instead, our attention is directed to the profusion of ear singing taking place during this period, which probably comprised the major thrust of the tradition. Could it have been eighty percent or more on a given night? Probably so.

While we may never know for sure how many early barbershoppers sang from a written script, nor how many relied solely upon oral tradition, we do know something about this dichotomy among barbershoppers in the United States today. Surely most would agree that nearly all what we hear, either on stage or at the afterglow, is the result of a printed arrangement, usually one that is well known to most barbershoppers across the country. Some music educators, perhaps, would look upon this positively, concluding that barbershoppers are more musically literate today than those of yesteryear, the supposition being that musical literacy is a good thing. When considering woodshedding, though, in the context of what we now know about world music, we are forced to be more thoughtful and critical in our analysis of improvisation, or for that matter, of any instance where music is transmitted by oral tradition.

Musical Literacy in the Western World

For centuries people from around the world have been struggling with the art of transcribing oral traditions as a means of preserving history and enabling it to be recreated, music included. Not only in the West, but in such diverse cultures as those of India, China, and pre-Columbian Mexico, attempts have been made with varying degrees of success to prescribe or depict music visually. Although it was a rather late achievement in recorded history, a very successful musical notation system was eventually developed in the western world that revolutionized European art music and was a major factor in setting it apart from the rest of the world's music.

The barbershop arrangements we look at today are the result of this long tradition of European note writing, based in part on medieval monks who put religious melodies called plainchants to parchment. (The leads, therefore, became literate before the rest of us!) In later centuries we start seeing evidence of partmusic for more than one voice, starting with organum and moving into other genres such as motets and madrigals. This visual notation enabled musicians to perform complex compositions, such as isorhythmic motets, which were not likely either to be improvised or to be performed by rote.

By the baroque period (roughly 1600–1750) the aristocratic music of Europe relied heavily, although not entirely, upon two five-line staves with black and white notes. Music theorists of the day began to write more and more about the distinctions between orally and visually transmitted music, and notation became so closely allied to musical composition that it eventually provided the basis for most performances of art music (see Sadie 1980:IX, 31–51).

The advantages of musical notation are obvious. Without it we might well be deprived of much beautiful music from earlier periods, such as Gregorian chants from the fourteenth century, the works of great composers such as Johann Sebastian Bach and George Frederick Handel, and perhaps even gems from the likes of a Harry Von Tilzer or an Ernest R. Ball. Unfortunately, it is common for the musically literate to reject orally transmitted music as something inferior to the notated variety. After generations of development in both language and musical literacy, numerous members of "learned" society in the Western world, particularly those specializing in literature and music, occasionally have rejected, both consciously and unconsciously, unwritten forms of literature and music as being somewhat less artful than those with visual prompts.

On the other side of the coin are those who believe that musical notation can be detrimental to the art of good music. I'm reminded here of someone who asked a seasoned banjo player if he could read music. "Not enough to hurt my playing" was the reply (Seeger, P. 1962:67). As amusing as that statement may be, there is a certain ring of truth in it. Many musicians and some musicologists believe that creativity can be imperiled by strict devotion to the printed page. It is only within the last century, and especially the last half century, that scholars studying folklore, anthropology, ethnomusicology and related disciplines have come to appreciate the value and sophistication of the oral transmission of culture.[1] Some of today's greatest orators, storytellers and masters of proverbs are found not in the so-called "civilized" societies of the western world, but among preliterate societies of developing nations. As societies "progress" to a state of literacy, something valuable and precious is often lost in the process. As people begin to rely upon the written word they become careless about the use of memory in recording cultural phenomena, or perhaps lazy in the approach to the transmission of the arts. Does this phenomenon have relevance to barbershop quartet singing? Maybe not, but some barbershoppers are wondering. In the barbershop quartet tradition, harmonic improvisation to a given melody was once the norm, while today most performances rely upon standard arrangements.

In the introduction to his book entitled *Improvisation: Its Nature and Practice in Music,* Derek Bailey sees the graphic notation of European music as being a detriment to many other kinds of world music. Could it have had the same effect upon woodshedding in the barbershop style?

> The petrifying effect of European classical music on those things it touches—jazz, many folk musics, and all popular musics have suffered grievously in their contact with it—made the prospect of finding improvisation there pretty remote. Formal, precious, self-absorbed, pompous, harbouring rigid conventions and carefully preserved hierarchical distinctions; obsessed with its geniuses and their timeless masterpieces, shunning the accidental and the unexpected; the world of classical music provides an unlikely setting for improvisation. (Bailey 1980:29)

Translated into a barbershop context, does this sound familiar? Does this help explain why some barbershoppers are still attracted to "winging it" in harmony, sometimes making more than a few musical mistakes in the process, when tidy arrangements, carefully mastered after hours of work by some of the finest arrangers in the Society, are readily available? It all has something to do with the euphoric nature of improvising that we can find not only in barbershopping, but in other genres of world music.

Improvisation and the Oral Transmission of Music

What is musical improvisation, then, and why is it important for barbershoppers to remain fluent in this creative art form? We can think of improvisation as spontaneous creativity during performance, within the accepted boundaries of a particular music culture, which can be perceived both by performers and listeners as an end product. It may be entirely new, but in most cases, it is the elaboration of an existing musical framework, element or elements, such as a melody. It is an ancient aspect of musical performance which is far older and more widespread, if we look at world music as a whole, than is musical performance that is prescribed by written notation. We should also remember that the appearance of multipart manuscripts does not coincide with the invention of choral harmony. To the contrary, part singing was around for centuries, indeed millennia, before written notes came on the scene.

> The spontaneous invention and shaping of music while it is being performed is as old as music itself. The very beginnings of musical practice can scarcely be imagined in any form other than that of instantaneous musical expression—of improvisation. . . . This joy in improvising while singing and playing is evident in almost all phases of music history. It was always a powerful force in the creation of new forms and every historical study that confines itself to the practical and theoretical sources that have come down to us in writing or print, without taking into account the improvisational element in living musical practice, must of necessity present an incomplete, indeed a distorted picture. For there is scarcely a single field in music that has remained unaffected by improvisation, scarcely a single musical technique or form of composition that did not originate in improvisatory practice or was not essentially influenced by it. The whole history of the development of music is accompanied by manifestations of the drive to improvise, though the element of improvisation retreats to the background in some phases, while in others it reveals a strikingly rich flowering. (Ferand 1961:5)

Polyphony as we know it today began as an improvised art form. Even among nobility and ecclesiastic leaders of Western Europe, harmonic vocal music was worked out in performance—improvised and preserved by rote—for centuries before written arrangements took hold. In the late fourteenth and early fifteen centuries it was common to improvise in parallel thirds above a "sighted" chant, something called gymel. In countries such as England, Germany, and Italy, the ancestral home of many present-day barbershoppers, harmonic improvisation was important both in and outside the church. Even throughout the baroque period, well after musical notation had taken hold, improvisation continued to be important in the music of the upper social classes as well as the peasantry. Spontaneous embellishment and decoration was the norm in just about any kind of music during this period in Europe.

Derek Bailey, quoted earlier, recognizes both the importance and the elusiveness of improvisation.

> Improvisation enjoys the curious distinction of being both the most widely practised of all musical activities and the least acknowledged and understood. While it is today present in almost every area of music, there is an almost total absence of information about it. Perhaps this is inevitable, even appropriate. Improvisation is always changing and adjusting, never fixed, too elusive for analysis and precise description; essentially non-academic. (Bailey 1980:1)

> But it still remains that one of the main effects of improvisation is on the performer, providing him with a creative involvement and maintaining his commitment. So, in those two functions, improvisa-

The Respectable Art of Woodshedding in World Music 41

tion supplies a way of guaranteeing the authenticity of the idiom, which also, avoiding the stranglehold of academic authority, provides the motor for change and continuous development. (Bailey 1980:28)

Just as some frown upon the oral transmission of music, Bailey points out the negative attitudes that improvisation brings to the devotees of some musical genres.

> Defined in any one of a series of catch-phrases ranging from 'making it up as he goes along' to 'instant composition', improvisation is generally viewed as a musical conjuring trick, a doubtful expedient, or even a vulgar habit. (Bailey 1980:1-2). . . . For it often seems to be the case that the extreme enthusiast resents improvisation and the unpredictable element it introduces, preferring the unchanging traditional aspects of his music. (Bailey 1980:4)

These statements will surely sound familiar to woodshedders.

The degree to which a musician improvises can vary from piece to piece, genre to genre, and from one oral tradition and music culture to another. Although most of the world's music, even today, is performed without the aid of written music, not all of that music can be classified as improvised. Much of the world's music is passed on orally with very little variation from one generation to another. In fact, in some cultures, a premium is placed on exact renditions of particular songs that are taught by one performer to another, much like a melody or the lead part is treated in barbershop quartet music. As the term woodshedding means different things to different people in barbershopping, so does the term improvisation carry different connotations both within and from one music culture to another.[2] Nevertheless, the meaning of the term is sufficiently universal to allow us a glimpse at harmonic improvisation in barbershopping as it relates to other kinds of world music.

Oral Traditions and Improvisation in Other Places

To help us appreciate the importance of oral transmission and improvisation in world music, let's leave the scene of Western art music and take a brief look at three musical traditions which encompass aspects of improvisation and oral transmission that can be compared to the art of barbershopping. The first two are quite unrelated to barbershopping. One is the folk tradition of southern Spain know as flamenco, and the other the classical music tradition of India. Finally, we will touch a third area of world music—Africa—which, unlike the other two, may have shared a role in shaping our own brand of improvisation. Our task here is not to analyze the myriad forms of musical improvisation found throughout the world, but to examine briefly other brands of world woodshedding, and in some cases see how performers and devotees conceptualize this remarkable performance practice.

In some European folk music improvisation has continued to be very important. Let's consider flamenco music for a moment, a genre familiar to many people in the United States, and one that some people feel has been transformed from folk music to a realm that is much too commercial. Although flamenco is not noted for its harmonic improvisation, improvisation is central to its melody, text, rhythm and dance. The comments of a well-known flamenco guitarist, Paco Pena, may be of some interest to those of us who improvise in the barbershop tradition.

> I'd say that within a piece you can reach certain heights because you have let yourself improvise, say, a little bit, not too much, but that little bit changes the whole character of the piece; in fact you might change perhaps a quarter of the piece, but that quarter changes the whole character of the whole piece.... The wonderful thing about this music is that you are completely free. You see, you feel so free because today you are going to play differently from yesterday. You are not tied by a composed piece which you have to play the same but better if you want to improve it. You could play much simpler—the piece could be less complicated, less elaborate and yet more subtle and therefore inspire you.... We have learned from our elders what they had learned from their elders. But we assimilate the music and treat it in our own way, as they did before. Flamenco is not a museum piece but a living developing art form, and as such it allows for the personal interpretation of the artists. (quoted in Bailey, 1980:26-28)

We find another parallel between flamenco and barbershopping in that both, in some respects, have "moved uptown" from the informal to the formal, losing something in the process as noted by Peter Manuel.

> The advent of the mass media has also contributed to rising technical standards, as musicians since the 1930s have been accustomed to studying and imitating recordings. Finally, as we have suggested, flamenco's professionalization and stylistic advances can be seen to some extent as the products of a self-conscious desire to dignify the art and thereby enhance the image of Andalusia and its gypsies.... Of course, there are many critics and aficionados who prefer the older,

The Respectable Art of Woodshedding in World Music 43

rougher, and allegedly more soulful styles of singing. . . . It is ironic, and yet not surprising, that "dignified" concert flamenco, in reaching out to a bourgeois and international audience, loses some of the characteristics which were most cherished and symbolically expressive to its native patrons. (Manuel 1989:57)

Barbershoppers, take note!
 Moving from Spain, let's take a brief sojourn to Asia, getting just about as far as possible, geographically speaking, from U.S. barbershopping. While improvisation plays a minor role in the art music of East Asian countries such as China, Japan and Korea, musical improvisation becomes more important in Southeast Asia, and is fundamental to the art music of India. Like a seasoned barbershop quartet woodshedder, a good improvisor in Asia is usually one who has been doing it for years, and has a maximum of experience and memorized passages upon which to draw. We are sometimes led to believe that good woodshedding is something that one is born with, something that does not require advanced preparation. In fact, a successful barbershop woodshedder is usually someone with a great deal of experience in anticipating chordal progressions, and one who contributes to the resolution of a chord on impact by making use of an impressive bank of harmonic memory. We can find our counterparts using similar techniques in many parts of the world, including Asia, where musical imagination leads to excellence in accepted art forms.

> An Asian musician usually spends many years memorizing and absorbing traditional models before he improvises, and his final rendering may well include fragments composed earlier.
>   In general, improvisation in Asian music requires imagination within the constraints of a framework in which particular musical elements are either obligatory, option or forbidden. It is largely the manipulation of the optional elements that marks the excellence of a musician. (Jairazbhoy 1980:52)

In India the test of a true musician cannot take place without a display of the creative ability to improvise. Much has been written on this aspect of Indian music, and many barbershoppers know something of the place of improvisation in Indian sitar performance because of the wide exposure that world-renowned sitarist Ravi Shankar has had in this country.[3]
 Even though four part harmony is not present in Indian classical music, the techniques of improvisation used in India would sound familiar to a classical woodshedder. An example would be

the following account by the Indian musician Viram Jasani, in which we could substitute his Indian Guru for our present day elder statesmen of woodshedding.

> The time that we spend with a Guru is purely spent in trying to understand the framework in which Indian music is set. And a Guru doesn't, or your teacher doesn't, really tell you how to improvise. That is purely up to the student to gain by experience and to intuit the various methods of playing the music. What he directly learns from his teacher is the framework in which improvisation or performance of Indian music takes place. But the teacher in Indian music is not usually an academic, he's not a theoretician, therefore a good teacher is able to show you and give you guidelines as to how to perform Indian classical music. He gives you the scope and the field in which to gain your experience and if you're a good student you take advantage of this opportunity that he gives you and then it becomes something that one develops on one's own. (quoted in Bailey 1980:16-17)

Closer to home is the improvisation that we find in the music of sub-Saharan Africa which has had a profound influence on all kinds of U.S. folk and popular musics. Here we consider a major tradition of world music that, unlike flamenco music and the art music of India, has played a direct role in shaping music in the United States.

Although it is more common to think of rhythm when contemplating African musical improvisation, this music takes us beyond spontaneous performance in rhythm and melody to improvisation in vocal harmony, comprising both harmonic polyphony and polyphony of a more contrapuntal nature, which is almost entirely of the oral tradition and seldom transcribed into Western notation. African performers do not usually think in terms of vertical chords as barbershop arrangers do, but rather of the simultaneous performance of two or more distinct melodies. What we would call harmony lines, such as the tenor or baritone parts, Africans would be more likely to call supporting melodies (Nketia 1974:160-167).

While we don't expect to hear barbershop chords being sung in traditional Africa, we do find traditional four-part (and sometimes more) harmonies being performed by some societies in sub-Saharan Africa (see Kauffman 1984). More common are two- and three-part societies in examples of vocal music, usually performed in a choral fashion, with many voices, rather than a vocal duet or trio (see Agawu 1990). Most important for consideration here,

The Respectable Art of Woodshedding in World Music

though, is the fact that much of this African vocal music is improvised.

> All these methods of harmonising may be employed simultaneously by members of the chorus. There is of course no apportioning of parts; singers choose to sing the primary response or sing something else against it. The effect of two or three parts is accordingly fortuitous in the sense that it would only arise where there were singers who felt like singing an upper part. (Nketia 1962:57)

From the early days of our colonial history, the Africans who came to North America brought with them their skills in musical improvisation and choral music, as did the people who came from Europe. Most of us already have some notion of how these two world traditions blended to form so many of our prsent genres, including gospel, blues, jazz, country music, rhythm and blues, rock 'n' roll, and others.

The number of African Americans engaged today in barbershop quartet music is relatively low, but as Africa has had considerable influence on the improvisational nature of various North American musical genres, there is reason to suspect that African Americans have played a role in the shaping of North American barbershopping harmony. An interesting analogy is the fact that it is also rare to find African American banjo players in the United States today, yet this uniquely North American musical instrument has its roots in Africa, and at one time was played primarily by people of African heritage.

The late Deac Martin, one of the prominent and early members of the Society, draws our attention to African influences on the barbershop tradition in his book entitled *Musical Americana* (Martin 1970:37–50). Although we hear few African American quartets today singing in barbershop style, such quartets, performing popular tunes of the barbershop variety, were definitely more prominent in pre-Society decades. We read in the autobiography of W. C. Handy that this well-known American musician traveled widely in the United States, singing popular songs in an African American vocal quartet, well before he became famous as a blues singer (Handy 1941:23–29). Another example comes to us from a note early this century in the Pittsburgh Press (24 August 1910): "Barber shop harmony by a black male quartet on Wylie Avenue cost four Negro youths of the Hill District." These four young men, whose names and addresses went down into history, were fined $3.00 each for harmonizing on the street!

Most of us are familiar with African American quartet singers, male and female, who perform both religious and pop music in styles somewhat related to barbershop. These people and their quartets have definitely influenced barbershop. It is not uncommon to meet senior barbershoppers who not only sang with African American woodshedders in pre-Society days, but who also were clearly influenced by quartets such as the Mills Brothers in their pursuit of harmonic improvisation.

Woodshedding in Early Society Years

While it is interesting to relate oral transmission and improvisation in barbershop style to other forms of world music, it is probably just as important to note that this style is different. Much of the improvisation mentioned above is both solo and instrumental. While harmonic improvisation is prevalent in other parts of the world, particularly in Africa and Europe, spontaneous four-part vocal harmony, one person to a part, is rare. Most improvisation does not encompass four musicians performing simultaneously; more often than not it is only one member of an ensemble improvising at any one time, and it is usually instrumental music, not vocal. Harmonic improvisation in barbershopping is both distinctive and sophisticated when viewed in the context of world music.

It is important to remember that the Society began as a woodshedding organization. When O. C. Cash and Rupert Hall, two acquaintances from Tulsa, ran into each other at the Kansas City Muelbach Hotel in early 1938, and scrounged up two strangers to sing baritone and bass with them, they weren't singing written arrangements; it was authenticity—harmony by ear. The first four men to show up at the Roof Garden of the Tulsa Club on 11 April 1938, including Cash and Hall, kicked off the evening by woodshedding "Down Mobile." No arrangements were sung that night either. Even at the "first roundup," the first national contest—Tulsa, Oklahoma, 1939, Bartlesville Fireflies and all—the name of the game was woodshedding.

As stated earlier, some quartets no doubt used arrangements well before 1938; bringing musical literacy to the Society was part of a natural progression of events that could not and should not have been prevented. Little by little, though, the formalization of the music through note reading and standard arrangements began to chip away at the need for improvisation. Cash, Hall and other founding members of the Society were well aware of this

The Respectable Art of Woodshedding in World Music 47

tension between the two approaches to quartet singing, and they all had mixed feelings on the subject. A review of early issues of *The Harmonizer*, the official magazine of the Society, gives some evidence of the soul-searching that went on during the first decade of the Society in trying to achieve a healthy balance between ear singing and note singing. One of the authors is none other than Sigmund Spaeth, a well-known scholar of music and devotee of barbershop quartet singing who published an edition entitled *Barber Shop Ballads* as early as 1924. In the May 1943 issue of *The Harmonizer* he writes:

> I insist that real barber shop harmony should either be actually extemporaneous or produce the effect of spontaneous improvisation. In that respect the art is a true branch of American folk-music. I would not have our harmonizers turn into an army of slavish note-readers; but I believe that the tricks of harmony can best be communicated from one quartet to another by the good old system of musical notation, and anyone who objects to written or printed music had better get a horse and carry his ideas around the country in Paul Revere style, for he is definitely behind the times. (*The Harmonizer*, Vol. 2, No. 4, May 1943, p. 6.)

Keep it spontaneous, he says, but don't ignore the benefits of musical literacy, keeping in mind that he was known for his musical literacy. As it would be interesting for us to go back in time and visit with the quartets of 1910, it would be equally interesting to have Sigmund Spaeth drop down and pass judgment on the art of harmonizing today. Would he find us to be "an army of slavish note-readers"? Probably so.[4]

One of the early champions of the Society to take pride in singing from arrangements, albeit their own handwritten arrangements, was the Elastic Four who won the national competition in 1942. All four members of this quartet had early training in music and much experience singing in church choirs. Their elegant spokesman and bass, Frank Thorne, was well-known among Society members. In an article entitled "How The Elastics Rehearse," Mr. Thorne makes his point clear:

> However, suppose we are about to tackle a new number. We are firm believers in writing out the parts, which task has been accomplished prior to rehearsal. When I hear about the aversion of some people to written music, I often wonder how well they remember addresses and telephone numbers if they do not write them down. (*The Harmonizer*, Vol. 4, No. 2, November 1944, p. 16.)

What Mr. Thorne fails to say here is that addresses and telephone numbers are hard to improvise with any success, yet for quartet singers, improvisation can produce spectacular results which can be retained in the musical memory from one rehearsal to the next.

Deac Martin was one of the most active Society members and prolific writers for *The Harmonizer*. He gave his ideas and opinions to its readers on a regular basis through his column entitled "The Way I See It." He and Frank Thorne were Society brothers, but did not always see eye to eye on key subjects. One of their more interesting discussions was on the subject of the annual national contest. Frank Thorne being strongly in favor, Deac Martin having certain reservations, preferring a parade of quartets rather than a contest. They each wrote letters to Society secretary Carroll Adams stating their positions, with Martin saying, in defense of the informality of the organization, "This should not be an organization of perfectionists, in my opinion" (*The Harmonizer*, Vol. 2, No. 4, May 1943, p. 18). On the subject of improvisation, Deac Martin was equally concerned that harmonizers might become too dependent on note reading, and his comments and those of others on the subject can be found in his regular column. In the first paragraph below he places some merit in the use of written arrangements, but in later columns he offers modest words of caution.

> In the early stages some of us were inclined to look sourly at quartets that had learned numbers by note rather than catch-as-catch-can. "It ain't barbershop," we said, because a lot of us thought of barbershopping as an unwritten agreement (maybe after the ninth attempt) on some swipe. In other words we thought of *method* and *atmosphere* as well as result. But these younger men have taught us a lot of harmony that we just didn't know existed. And now these harmonies are down in black and white so that any quartet that's willing to work can learn them. Furthermore, they're on the record for future generations.
>
> As long as he sticks to main principles—tenor above lead 99% of the time, and basses below—Leopold Stokowsky can write barbershop arrangements for me if he wants to. But, when Don Webster, Joe Wolff, Phil Embury and those like us get together, we'll probably change 'em in spots to "the way they OUGHT to be sung." ("Drop a note on that, Cy."). And then, if it sounds good enough for future use, I'll laboriously *write it down*. That's the way I see it. (*The Harmonizer*, Vol. 3, No. 2, December 1943, p. 8)

The Respectable Art of Woodshedding in World Music 49

Discovered—one (1) reader of this col. Cy Perkins loudly cheers the recommendation made in Sept. issue that notes are invaluable for chorus work (purely ghastly in early stages without 'em), to show how somebody else sings a number, and for use by us in self-improvement but agrees that too frequent use of little black dots causes degeneration of the inner ear, or wherever the sense-of-harmony is located. (*The Harmonizer*, Vol. 4, No. 2, November 1944, p. 24)

The way I see it, we've got to watch our step or we'll lose the original trail blazed by the founders and later developed in a well paved road to Informal Harmonyland. I refer to too frequent use of notes.

When we set up an Arrangement Committee it was for the purpose of getting on paper the arrangements as sung by this-'n-that quartet, and also to develop arrangements as a guide to harmonious effects. We said then, and we still believe, that Society arrangements are necessary. But, as Phil Embury has repeated so often, they are sent with the hope that each quartet will put something of its self into the arrangement. Our arrangements are invaluable in group singing and in showing a new quartet or a new chapter what is good barbershop harmony.

But, too often nowadays in our meeting, we pick a quartet at random from the members, stand 'em up in front, and tell 'em to give. Then, the four fumble around on "What'll we sing"—and end up by singing a Society arrangement pretty exactly as written, rather than "Sweet Sue," "Girl in the Heart of Maryland," "Tell Me Why," or some other good old number, barging into it and letting the notes fall where they will.

It's natural that any four men singing for an audience want to do as good a job as possible. But, along with singing arranged music, let's tear into the good old-timers often, catch-as-catch-can, and by impromptu trial and error develop their harmony possibilities. . . .

Our arrangements are splendid. We must have them. But, let's not use them as a crutch. Let's not lose the spirit of adventure. Owen Cash exemplifies that, to me. "Let's try it this way," sezzhe, and without embarrassment because somebody may be listening, they try it, and get the thrill of discovery. . . .

Let's not get soft in the ability to explore and work out stuff that sounds good to us regardless of what those scoffers on the sidelines may say. . . . (*The Harmonizer*, Vol. 4, No. 1 September 1944, p. 10)

In the same issue of *The Harmonizer* as above there is a piece entitled "Judges Will Look and Listen At Detroit . . . But Mostly Listen." It gives an interesting perspective on the reason for having Society arrangements.

As to giving credit to a quartet that uses a "Society arrangement" and adds a few original touches of its own, as against using the "Society arrangement" straight, the former quartet would be rated highest for the reason that all society arrangements are only designed as a good point from which to start and variation should be encouraged. (*The Harmonizer*, Vol. 4, No. 1, March 1944, p. 4)

About six months after Frank Thorne's article on the importance of written arrangements for his 1942 champion quartet, Leo Ives described how his 1943 champion quartet the Four Harmonizers rehearse. It is more in keeping with the woodshedding school of most of the winning quartets of the early days of national competition, as is the subsequent excerpt by J. George O'Brien about his less competitive Slap Happies quartet.

> Four Harmonizers:
> When we have selected a number to learn, I usually sing the lead, if I know it, or I learn it from one of the boys who does know the melody. The rest of the boys extemporize or fake their harmony parts for the first few phrases (probably about 8 bars of that stuff they call "music.") (*The Harmonizer*, Vol. 4, No. 4, May 1945, p. 13)

> Slap Happies:
> In addition to our other handicaps, none of us reads music. . . . We just keep right on singing the same songs, but we never sing them twice alike. (*The Harmonizer*, Vol. 5, No. 1, August 1945, p. 34)

We never sing them twice alike—one of the important reasons why woodshedders take such great delight in their art. The sense of surprise by a new chord or a new series of chords never fails to enchant the zealous woodshedder in a way that somehow surpasses the entertainment of a well-sung arrangement, with perfect chord executions and progressions. The euphoric sensation of woodshedding may have something to do with the perception of creativity in which musical improvisers around the world revel. This is another subject worthy of pursuit, but one that time does not allow us to embark upon here.

Conclusions

Woodshedding in barbershop style is an oral tradition utilizing musical improvisation, and should be viewed as a viable and respectable art form in the context of world music. Improvisation was once a very important component in European art music, and there are some who feel that something was lost in the almost complete conversion from oral improvisation to literacy in Western art music. Even in the Spanish folk genre of flamenco, which is still basically an improvisational art form, there is some fear that a wane in improvisation will be detrimental to the tradition. In India, to the contrary, improvisation is still an important force in its art music, one of the most widely respected music traditions in the world today. Africa is another of the great improvisatory sources of world music, and one that has had a direct impact upon North American music.

Woodshedding is presently in a state of decline, and there are barbershoppers today who feel that this mode of performance is not a flattering feature of barbershopping. Conversely, there are those who think that woodshedding is worth preserving and promoting. The Ah-Sow organization (Ancient & Harmonious Society of Woodshedders, Ltd.) was formed in 1978 to do for woodshedding much the same job that the Society was formed to do for barbershopping in general back in 1938. This organization has a woodshedding method in print, and is presently in the process of producing a new version. In 1982 the first annual Pioneer Weekend of pure woodshedding took place, and it now is held every September in Chicago. In 1988 a similar weekend was promoted in Baltimore and its followers continue to meet there every February. The quarterly publication of the GUBOS Group (Give Us Back Our Society) first came out in September of 1987 and continues to give us letters from around the country written by people plugging the woodshedding idea. Similar sentiments can also be found on a regular basis in letters to the editors of *The Harmonizer,* as well as district and chapter publications. This enthusiasm for woodshedding is combined with a sense of realism on the part of the promoters. Few of them expect or really desire a return to the "good old days," throwing their printed arrangements to the wind and constantly pining for an unarranged melody. Instead, they are trying to garner respect for a dying but worthy brand of barbershopping not widely appreciated by most members of today's Society, but a performing style they believe to be more of an asset than a detriment to the future of the tradition and the Society.

In the art music of the Western World today there is a movement for authenticity in the performance of music from earlier centuries—sometimes called the Historical Performance Movement—that has people performing music on instruments of the period, even though instruments of today are technically superior.[5] Playing horns, fiddles and flutes of earlier design produces a somewhat different sound, one that would have been familiar to Johann Sebastian Bach and his contemporaries. Here too we have debates. If Bach were around today, would he prefer the old or the new sound? We will never know, but there is certainly a way to please both camps, and that is to foster both methods of performance.

In the same movement we find musicians reverting to former vocal techniques, not as familiar and acceptable to modern ears, creating singing that more closely represents the performance sound of the composer's day. Proponents of this movement find it to be a refreshing departure from the slickness and commercialization of most performances of art music heard today, as do the proponents of woodshedding in barbershopping today. There certainly is room for both types of performance practice today, in barbershopping as well as in Western art music.

The future of woodshedding is closely tied to the perseverance of barbershopping in general, and while optimism abounds on the part of some, there are also signs of disappointment ahead. One of the requisites to forecasting the endurance of barbershopping in general, and woodshedding in particular, is understanding the transition that is presently taking place in the Society from contextual to non-contextual performers. Here we can distinguish between those members of the Society who grew up harmonizing songs they commonly heard within the context of their childhood, and those of more recent birth who learned this music out of context, almost exclusively through the Society. An exception would be the children of Society members who heard this music, sometimes from infancy, through the involvement of their parents in the Society. The vast majority of those calling for a revival of woodshedding belong to the first category, the contextual folks, and within fifty years or so none of them will be around.[6]

Can the non-contextual group, brought up mostly on slick arrangements, ever get good enough at woodshedding to appreciate its value? If present practice is any indication of the outcome, the prospects are not very hopeful; barbershopping has become too formal, technical and commercial to nurture woodshedding organically. However, if the younger generation of barbershoppers can be convinced of the value of oral transmission and harmonic improvisation in barbershop style, there might be room for optimism. Hundreds of contextual woodshedders are just dying to pass on their beloved tradition.

Notes

1. For a discussion of this subject from a global perspective please see *The Oral and the Literate in Music,* Yosihiko and Osamu, eds., 1986.
2. For an interesting discussion on the many meanings of improvisation please see "Thoughts on Improvisation: A Comparative Approach", Nettl, 1974.
3. For a rather detailed account of the place of improvisation in the art music of India please see Powers 1980.
4. Spaeth's claim that improvisation makes barbershop quartet music "a true branch of American folk music" is interesting. The eminent American musicologist Charles Seeger, among others, has defined this music not as folk music but as popular music, and rightfully so if we focus on the origin of the melodies themselves (Seeger, C. 1980:445). We must also look, though, at performance practice. Perhaps Seeger was not considering the improvisational side of quartet singing when he wrote on this subject. Spaeth is certainly correct in classifying quartet woodshedding as a form of traditional American folk music.
5. See *Authenticity and Early Music,* Kenyon, 1988.
6. This dilemma is at the heart of the membership problem being faced today by the Society, but one that is seldom recognized or discussed. The pool of people who grew up hearing barbershop harmony in its natural context, apart from Society influence, continues to shrink and within a number of decades will be gone.

References

Agawu, V. Kofi. "Variation Procedures in Northern Ewe Song." Ethnomusicology, Vol. 34, No. 2, Spring/Summer 1990, pp. 221–43.

Bailey, Derek. Improvisation: Its Nature and Practice in Music. Ashbourne, Derbyshire: Moorland Publishing Co. Ltd., 1980. 154 pp.

Encyclopedia Britannica, "barbershop quartet", "B" Volume, p. 807, 1978.

Ferand, E. T. (ed.) Improvisation in Nine Centuries of Western Music. Cologne: Arno Volk Verlag, 1961. 163 pp.

Handy, W. C. Father of the Blues. New York: The Macmillan Company, 1941. xv, 317pp.

Jairazbhoy, Nazir A. "Improvisation" (Asian Art Music), The New Grove Dictionary of Music and Musicians, Vol. 9, pp. 52–6, 1980.

Kauffman, Robert A. "Multipart Relationships in Shona Vocal Music" in Nketia, J. H. Kwabena and Jacqueline Cogdell DjeDje, Eds., Selected Reports in Ethnomusicology, Vol. V, Studies in African Music, Los Angeles: UCLA Department of Music, 1984. 385 pp.

Kenyon, Nicholas, Ed. Authenticity and Early Music: A Symposium. New York: Oxford University Press, 1988. 219 pp.

Manuel, Peter. "Andalusian, Gypsy, and Class Identity in the Contemporary Flamenco Complex." Ethnomusicology, Vol. 33, No. 1, Winter 1989, pp. 47–65.

Martin, Claude Trimble (Deac). Book of Musical Americana. Englewood Cliffs: Prentice-Hall, Inc., 1970. 243 pp.

Nettl, Bruno. "Thoughts On Improvisation: A Comparative Approach." The Musical Quarterly, Vol. LX, No. 1, January 1974, pp. 1–19.

Nketia, J. H. Kwabena. African Music in Ghana. Accra: Longmans, 1962. 148 pp.

Nketia, J. H. Kwabena. The Music of Africa. New York: W. W. Norton and Company, Inc., 1974. 278 pp.

Pittsburgh Press, 24 August 1910.

Powers, Harold S. "India" (Improvisation), The New Grove Dictionary of Music and Musicians, Vol. 9, pp. 107–13, 1980.

Sadie, Stanley, ed. The New Grove Dictionary of Music and Musicians. Washington, DC: Grove's Dictionaries of Music Inc., 1980.

Seeger, Charles. "United States of America" (Folk Music), The New Grove Dictionary of Music and Musicians, Vol. 19, pp. 436–47, 1980.

Seeger, Peter. How To Play The 5-String Banjo. Beacon, N.Y., 1962. Third Edition. 72pp.

Yosihiko, Tokumaro and Yamaguit Osamu, eds. The Oral and the Literate in Music. Tokyo: Academica Music, 1986. xi, 484 pp.

Becoming a Barbershop Singer

ROBERT A. STEBBINS

They call themselves "barbershoppers." They sing an indigenous American music, with roots in classical and popular song that led in the late 1800s to the practice of men singing in barbershops. Today the barbershoppers are organized into three international societies: the all-male Society for the Preservation and Encouragement of Barbershop Quartet Singing in America (SPEBSQSA) and the all-female Sweet Adelines International and Harmony, Inc. (a late 1950s offshoot of Sweet Adelines). Interest in barbershop singing, or "barbershopping," has been expressed not only in quartets, which are, nonetheless, the oldest form of the art, but also for several decades in choruses. The interest has been spreading beyond the borders of the United States since approximately 1950, chiefly to countries where English is the mother tongue or a major second language. There are presently about 35,000 women and 40,000 men in barbershop organizations around the world, with the strongest international development of the art still to be found in Canada.

Barbershoppers are organized locally into chapters the main goal of which is to promote choral and quartet singing in barbershop style: "unaccompanied vocal music characterized by consonant four-part harmony for every melody note [in which] occasional brief passages may be sung by fewer than four voice parts" (SPEBSQSA, 1980:3). The typical chorus meets weekly in an evening rehearsal. Members of the chorus who are also members of a quartet commonly rehearse with the latter group during another evening. Maturity in choral and quartet singing means, among other things, that these groups strive for a level of excellence such that they can attract the public to annual shows and shorter concerts of various kinds known within barbershop circles as "singouts." Even more demanding in terms of polish is competing in annual regional (female) or district (male) contests where panels of highly trained judges evaluate and rank each quartet and chorus in attendance. Winners advance to the ultimate competition, that held subsequently at an international convention of their society.

This is the core of barbershopping. The enjoyment of singing music in barbershop style is the central reason for participating in this form of leisure. There are, in addition, numerous activities involving many members that, although peripheral in the sense that they are not music making, are nonetheless important as support for it. Thus members may participate in the administrative affairs of their chapter and region or district and, more rarely, of their international society. Costumes and uniforms are worn at contests and performances, which members must either make or purchase. Annual shows are often presented in front of a theatrical backdrop of some sort; this is constructed by the singers. Prospective members must be first recruited and then auditioned, new music ordered and distributed, and periodic workshops for individual and collective improvement organized, all tasks that fall to certain committees. Still other committes are responsible for show publicity, ticket sales, and social events. The latter include the annual banquets, Christmas parties, and "afterglows," or the lively and lengthy receptions for insiders held after each show, that are centered on ample food, drink, conversation, and of course, quartet singing. A barbershopper can become heavily immersed in all this and more if he or she chooses to do so; it can become *a* main or *the* main leisure activity in that person's life.

The aim of this chapter is to explore how a sample of Canadian men and women became attracted to this artistic core and its peripheral activities. The data come from an exploratory-qualitative study of the quartets and choruses of three chapters in Calgary, Alberta as well as a small male splinter group that holds a "license" as a chapter in the process of developing. One main source of data was participation observation of the main activities of the chapters and the splinter group, which included travelling with them to their regional or district conventions.

The other main source was a set of unstructured interviews with thirty-two singers: a representative sample from two of the four chapters consisting of sixteen males (eight in quartets, eight in choruses) and sixteen females (same distribution). The data were collected by the author over the fourteen-month period running from December 1988 to January 1990. The decision to use exploratory methodology to study barbershop, and thereby to develop a grounded theory of it, is justified by the total absence of sociological data on the subject.

Barbershop Singing as Serious Leisure

One principal conclusion to come from the aforementioned study is that barbershop is, for the majority of both the male and the female samples, a form of serious leisure. This is its scientific classification. Serious leisure is the systematic pursuit of an amateur, hobbyist, or volunteer activity that is substantial enough for the participant to find a career there in the acquisition and expression of its special skills or knowledge or both. The question of whether serious leisure is genuine leisure is addressed elsewhere (Stebbins, 1992a, Chapter 1). Here I shall deal only with its six distinguishing qualities and its various types.

Serious leisure is leisure in which participants encounter the occasional need to persevere, although it is encountered significantly less often than in some occupations and significantly more often than in its opposite, casual leisure. As mentioned, there is a career to be found in serious leisure, which consists of a history of turning points, stages of achievement and involvement, and a set of background contingencies. Third, personal effort based on extensive knowledge, training, or skill and sometimes a combination of these is common in such leisure. Various durable benefits are derived from it, including self-actualization, self-enrichment, feelings of group accomplishment, and self-image enhancement. Further, one finds associated with each serious leisure activity a unique ethos composed of special beliefs, norms, values, morals, events, principles, and traditions. These five qualities are the soil in which the sixth distinguishing quality takes root: participants come to identify strongly with their avocation.

Amateurs make up one category of serious leisure participant. They are defined by their many interdependent relationships with a professional counterpart and a public who is served by either or both sets of experts (see Stebbins, 1979, for more details on this definition). The second category of serious leisure participant—the career volunteer—engages in voluntary action (action that is uncoerced and not primarily aimed at remuneration) that helps others and is thereby deemed beneficial (Van Til, 1979). For them volunteering is an enduring expression of skill or knowledge or both.[1] Moreover, career volunteers are driven chiefly by altruistic motives rather than by the self-interest that motivates amateurs and, as we shall see shortly, hobbyists. The volunteers also carry out as leisure tasks that are delegated to them by certain superiors employed in the organization in which they serve.

An important difference between hobbyists and amateurs is that the first lie outside the professional-amateur-public systems of our society. Hobbyists are also less likely to have publics, and they never have professional counterparts (although there may be a commercial counterpart, Stebbins, 1992a). Hobbyists come in four categories: there are collectors of things (e.g., paintings, stamps, old cars) about which one must develop a technical knowledge if one is to succeed at and enjoy this form of leisure. There are makers of and tinkerers with the various complex artifacts of our age (e.g., furniture makers, lapidary workers, handicrafters). The activity participant pursues a form of leisure for the development and expression of skills or knowledge and for the personal enrichment these offer. Here we find those engaged in bodybuilding, watching birds, and square dancing. The fourth category of hobbyist is the player of games or sports, rule-based contests for which there is no true professional equivalent (as defined sociologically) such as we find in the amateur world (e.g., horseshoes, archery, canoe racing, cross-country running).

Barbershop singing is a hobby and those who pursue it are activity participants. There is no profession of barbershop singing that can meet the definitional criteria of profession used by certain sociologists (c.f., Pavalko, 1988: Chapter 2). A handful of quartets, notably the Buffalo Bills, who appeared in Meredith Wilson's *The Music Man,* and the Dapper Dans at Disney World and Disneyland, have worked full-time for several years, but they do not amount to a profession. Over ninety-nine percent of barbershoppers pursue their art as serious leisure, even though the leading quartets are highly polished and entertaining, good enough to command substantial fees at numerous singouts and be invited as headliners for district, regional, and national conventions. Indeed, the top quartets and choruses are said by barbershop singers to be of professional quality, although lacking a true profession and hence a professional standard against which to measure all performances this is an empty claim.

The Barbershop Career

Careers are found in serious leisure as in work and in other major life identities. That is, there is in each form of serious leisure a distinctive set of background conditions and factors that helps explain how the novice gets launched there. As in all careers, there are also special contingencies in the serious leisure career, chance encounters and events that propel the participant toward different kinds of involvements. In addition there are various turning points, or new directions in the leisure career, which are influenced significantly less by chance than by personal effort. Finally, there is always a motivational component to be considered, treated here under the headings of thrills and disappointments in barbershop singing. Missing in most, if not all, serious leisure careers are the career stages that we so often find in the world of work. Still continuity and movement, the essence of any career, are assured in the patterns of contingencies and turning points that serious leisure participants invariably pass through.

BACKGROUND

Many of the men and women sampled had only a dim awareness of barbershop prior to their first direct contact with it. Their image of it, typically, was one of quartets, perhaps inspired by watching *The Music Man*. Often the precontact image was neutral, even unflattering. As a consequence, very few respondents said that they made the first move in the string of events that led to joining a barbershop chapter. Rather it was an active barbershopper who, in the majority of cases, invited the respondent to an annual show or choral rehearsal (but never to a quartet rehearsal). This chance meeting between prospective singer and chapter member is the first contingency in the barbershop career.

Approximately two-thirds of the men and women sampled were encouraged by a barbershop friend or acquaintance to attend an annual show or choral rehearsal. This pattern is probably not unique to Calgary, since many respondents were living elsewhere in Canada at the time. Relatives played a small role in this sample; four men were invited by a relative whereas no woman was.[2] One man and four women sought out the local chapter on their own, either by making inquiries in their church choirs or by responding to a newspaper notice about the group.

The large majority of both samples was motivated by a special "leisure lack" (Neulinger, 1981: 188–91): insufficient opportunity to sing choral music. For a minority of this group, this lack was total; there were no singing opportunities whatsoever. Most respondents, however, were in church choirs at the time, from which they developed a craving for more and sometimes better singing outlets. These singers hoped to find in the barbershop chorus what many barbershop veterans already know, namely, that it is likely to be more demanding and therefore of higher musical quality than a number of church choirs.

Despite the motivational state created by the special lack of choral leisure, only half of each sample joined the local chapter within a month or two of initial contact. Shortage of time for the new leisure was the most common reason for this delay, which sometimes lasted several years. For these respondents there were children to raise or a paid job to fulfill. Their wish to join the world of close harmony was not, however, frustrated by competing leisure interests. Moreover, a few of those who failed to take up the art more or less on the spot had moved from the community where the initial exposure took place or were exposed to barbershop outside the community in which they lived, but in which there was no barbershop.

The findings that relatives played a small role in bringing members of the two samples into the realm of barbershop, when compared with friends and acquaintances, can be explained in part by another finding, which is that few relatives were themselves former or current barbershoppers. Only six of the thirty-two respondents reported encouragement from a relative who was in barbershop (four men, two women). A couple of other respondents said they later discovered barbershoppers in their extended families, revelations that came from talk about their own involvements. Indeed, the families of the respondents were generally unmusical. Family members seldom seriously sang or played musical instruments.

Still this was hardly true for the respondents themselves. Two-thirds of each sample was singing or had sung in a church choir. And the women, in particular, had other kinds of musical involvements often stretching back to childhood. Nine of them, compared with three men, had been in high school glee clubs. Four women had taken voice lessons, seven had taken lessons on a musical instrument. No man had received voice lessons, whereas only three had studied on a musical instrument. Thus, it is hardly surprising that twice as many women as men (ten compared with five) said they could read music well enough to learn new barbershop songs by this method alone.

It is of note that only one member of each sample had sung in a community chorus. To the extent that such groups sing classical music, they may hold little appeal for the typical barbershopper, who certainly likes light fare. But the widespread inability to read music also prevents him or her from joining a community chorus. To be able to read music is an advantage insofar as it helps a singer to learn a part quickly or sing that part immediately when encountered as new music. Yet "ear singing," which amounts to learning a part by hearing it sung repeatedly, and "woodshedding," or improvising, are traditions in barbershop, although the second is rare among women. Barbershop got its start among men who liked to sing, but whose talents were typically undeveloped. They had untrained voices, they could read no music, but the music was also simple enough harmonically to allow woodshedding by those who provided the harmony parts. The growing emphasis on learning parts has tended to make this practice less and less respectable.

GETTING INVOLVED

Besides attending choral rehearsals and singing in shows, contests, and singouts, which is the minimal level of participation, newly recruited barbershoppers have three additional involvements open to them: joining or forming a quartet, developing as a singer, and performing service work. The first two are typical of hobbies everywhere; they offer an opportunity to pursue a substantial personal interest that is self-actualizing and self-expressive. The third, by contrast, calls on the altruistic spirit of the barbershopper to serve his or her art as a volunteer.

Turning to the prospect of joining or forming a quartet, it was found that most respondents, although somewhat more women (twelve) than men (nine), developed an interest in this aspect of barbershop only after they had joined a chapter. Five men, however, had quartet singing in mind when they went as guests to their first rehearsal. For those whose fascination with quartet singing came later, this new orientation took anywhere from one to fifteen to twenty years to germinate. Still, most respondents were recruited to a quartet or formed one of their own within three to five years of entry into barbershop.

Getting involved in a quartet is, in many ways, an imprecise undertaking. Because this type of singing is quite exposed (no one else has the same part), many respondents spoke of an initial lack of confidence in their ability to perform in this manner. Some accepted with reluctance invitations to join a quartet. Others experimented with quartet singing by attending jam session-like evenings with friends. A few of the men acquired a taste for it at one of the novice quartet nights sponsored by the chapter. On these occasions anyone can organize a quartet for the purpose of performing a tune or two before other chapter members.

Even after the singer has become committed to the idea of quartet singing, implementing it is usually problematic to some degree. It is a challenge to find four men or women who are willing to devote an additional four hours a week to rehearsing (beyond rehearsing with the chorus), whose voices have an acceptable blend, who can get along with each other, and who can agree on goals for the group, to mention a few of the possible obstacles. Being recruited to an established quartet often skirts these problems, but opens the singer up to others. Established quartets may lose members through transfers at work, surges in occupational or domestic responsibility, changes in leisure interests, or pressure from a spouse who feels the singer is devoting too much time to the art. In short, quartet singing is always a struggle of one sort or another, which, as I indicate elsewhere (Stebbins, 1992b), is nevertheless well worth the effort.

Self-actualization and self-expression are two of the many rewards to be gained from quartet singing. But they are possibly even more rewarding when gained through the process of singing development, which occurs in many different ways, only some of which are discussed here. For the women, it was possible to receive short sessions of personal vocal instruction (PVI). Here a more or less untrained barbershopper is tutored by a comparatively well-trained member of the same chorus in the techniques of singing (e.g., breathing, posture, muscle control, mouth formation), as well as perhaps in how to sing the songs on which the chorus is presently working. At present the men have no equivalent of PVI. Still, Mel Knight (1991), director of music education and services for SPEBSQSA, notes that PVI is available in some men's groups, but that, in his experience, it is a relatively uncommon service for both sexes.

Both the men and the women held occasonal weekend workshops prior to annual shows and contests to improve the critical aspects of choral performance. These events were invariably led by one or more experts, a well-known and experienced coaches from SPEBSQSA or Sweet Adelines International or respected members of the chapter. The aspects worked on over the two days were many and varied, among them harmony, pronunciation of words in songs,[3] dynamics (transitions from loud to soft and vice versa), and balance of melodic and harmonic lines. An important consideration in these sessions was stage presence (in men's groups) or choreography (in women's groups): the facial and bodily gestures and movements that are designed to enhance the presentation and meaning of the song being sung. Frowning, smiling, raising the arms, and shifting position on the risers are examples. Members of the front line of a chorus may leave their positions to do unison maneuvers on the stage floor, or an event may be enacted there, such as pitching a baseball to a batter and catcher (complete with props) to embellish the singing of "Take Me Out To The Ball Game."

Further, the women mix the goals of PVI and the workshops in regional retreats held largely to improve the singing capacity of those in attendance. In this instance there is no show or contest for which to prepare, for singers come to the retreat from different chapters in the area. Instruction is collective and organized around a visiting expert or two. The nearest equivalent among the Calgary men is to attend the week-long Harmony College held each summer in Missouri. Here students take courses in quartet singing, ear training, sight-reading, song arranging, and other specialities. Music and performance experts also travel to the chapters to assist with show production and give instruction in music skills, and additional instruction is sometimes available in district training sessions.

The three ways of self-improvement on the choral level are found, in a sense, on the quartet level, although only among those singers in seriously-minded units. The quartets whose goal is to compete in contests or perform at singouts and annual shows are always striving to improve. The mere act of singing in such a group on a weekly basis brings a certain rate of improvement. In addition the group is likely to have a coach, a local, expert male or female singer (to coach quartets of either sex) whose job is to advise on such musical matters as balance, pronunciation, and harmony. Since stage presence and choreography are also important facts of quartet singing, the coach may be asked to comment here as well.

Finally, the choruses and quartets competing at regional and district contests receive evaluations from panels of judges. The judges are meticulously trained by their respective societies to evaluate one of four aspects of barbershop singing. Although different names are given to these aspects, they refer to the same notions: the musical arrangement of the song, the vocal production of the song (e.g., balance, harmony), the interpretation given the song, and the showmanship, or stage presence, with which the song is presented. The judges' comments are widely respected. They can thus serve as a basis for personal and group improvement.

Service work, the third major way of getting further involved after joining a chorus, is clearly more altruistic than the first two ways. The following partial list of committees and positions indicates the breadth of service that can be rendered: executive, annual show, wearing apparel, music (selection of songs, auditions), section leader (of basses, baritones, etc.), chapter bulletin editor, and public relations. There appears to be as many opportunities of this sort for the women as for the men.

Volunteer help is always welcome, and the appeal for it also comes from higher organizational levels. Regional, district, and international duties are there to be filled, including representing one's chapter at the next level, administering business there, and becoming certified as a judge. There are also a number of informal tasks, such as setting up risers, coordinating social activities, picking up visiting coaches and quartets at the airport, and making audiotapes of song parts as learning aids.

The service component of the barbershop career tended to begin within the first two to three years of joining the chapter. Perhaps it would have been possible to delay this turning point still further, but many newcomers were eager to gain acceptance and learn from the inside how the chapter functioned. All but a handful of respondents said their service involvement (formal and informal) was either moderate or heavy. That is, they worked on at least one major committee or assignment equal in time to attending a second rehearsal each week. Quartet members were as active in this regard as nonquartet, choral members. Family or work obligations or both sometimes restricted the amount of service a singer could offer, but the expectation that all will help in this area was strongly felt by every respondent.

Self-development as a singer is part of the subjective side of the barbershop career (Stebbins, 1970) in the sense that the person can discern growing improvement and involvement over the years. Service work fits into the subjective barbershop career as one of its turning points: entry into still another part of the barbershop lifestyle. With it comes a feeling of belonging and an opportunity for sociability with like-minded avocational colleagues.

PARTICIPANTS AND DEVOTEES

Yet, involvement in singing, in development of singing capacity, and in service work is far from uniform. Some barbershoppers are clearly more immersed in their serious leisure than others. In barbershop, as in the amateur-professional pursuits I studied (e.g., Stebbins, 1982; 1984), there are participants and devotees.

Thus, in this study too, the devotees are highly dedicated to the hobby of barbershop, whereas the participants are only moderately dedicated, but significantly more so than players or dabblers in it.

The sampling procedure used in this study lent itself poorly to any attempt to estimate the proportions of participants and devotees in the Calgary chapters. The decision to draw equal samples of quartet and choral singers gave more numerical weight in those samples to the former than they actually have in a typical barbershop chapter. Therefore, I can only indicate the lines along which participants and devotees are separated in this art. Most of the main dimensions have already been suggested; they are service work, individual practice at home, choral and quartet singing (rehearsals, shows, contests, singouts), and singing development (PVI, workshops, retreats, Harmony College).

In the past studies of amateurs, the participants have tended to be those who are more or less steadily involved in the core and at least some of the peripheral activities of the pursuit as measured by standards of involvement that prevail there. In barbershop, the participants are those who attend most choral rehearsals and sessions for vocal and choral development, sing in the annual show, and go to the regional or district convention and contest each year. Participants here also shoulder a moderate service load. By these criteria, most men and women in barbershop are participants, a proportion that is typical of amateurs as well.

Devotees are likely to attend somewhat more faithfully the choral rehearsals and developmental sessions and are substantially more likely to be in a busy quartet or be highly active in service work or both. For the men, attending Harmony College, because of the time and financial commitment this entails, is sufficient to win them the label of devotee at this point in their leisure careers. Devotees spend considerably more than the average amount of time at home practicing singing in general and learning parts in particular. Participants are inclined to do significantly less of this.

Participant hobbyists shade off into nonhobbyists, referred to in the theory as dabblers or players. Dabblers *play* around at barbershop, treating it as casual rather than as serious leisure, as measured, for example, by low rehearsal attendance and a failure to learn their parts. Serious-minded chapters try to rid themselves of these members if the members fail to sense that much more is expected of them than they are prepared to give and leave the chapter of their own accord. All Calgary chapters have rules about attendance at choral rehearsals; poor attendance leads to the cancellation of membership unless there are extenuating circumstances. The pressure to attend is highest starting four to five rehearsals before a contest or annual show.

CAREER HIGH POINTS

Each respondent was asked to identify the thrills, or high points, in his or her barbershop career. These events are important because they motivate the singer to stick with the art in hope of finding similar experiences again, demonstrate that diligence and commitment can pay off, and serve as major turning points in the leisure career. Although chance plays a role in the outcome of thrilling events, a barbershopper still has a significant degree of control over the outcome if the event is regarded as a high point and not as a career contingency. This is evident in the following high points listed by the respondents, which were the same for both sexes.

By far the most important high point, as measured in terms of frequency of mention in the interviews, was competing or winning as a chorus or quartet in a regional, district, or international contest. As an experience, this high point refers to being swallowed up in a sea of barbershop song, in a sea of pure, ringing, consonant harmonies to which the audience responds with avid appreciation. These conditions—the production of the song and its reception—are most commonly joined at contests, where chorus members are most likely to concentrate to the fullest, motivated by the possibility of winning or at least placing well.

No other high point discussed in the interviews came close to this one in terms of personal impact and frequency of mention. Singing to any appreciative audience (not just one at a contest) and performing singouts as a quartet were tied as the second most prominent thrill. It is safe to conclude that singing well before any "good" audience—that is, one that likes the music—is what barbershop singers come to live for in their serious leisure.

The disappointments found in barbershop tell us something indirectly about its high points. The women much more than the men (ten respondents to four) listed an unexpectedly low placement in a contest with reference to their group's goals as their first and often sole disappointment. It is a thrill to sing in contests, but one of the risks of the pursuit of this thrill is failure, that is, low placement. And it is possible at both the chorus and the quartet levels to sing well but place in the middle of the list of contestants, for competition is intense at regional or district conventions and even more so at "international."

A quarter of each sample described the low commitment of certain members of the chapter—borderline or full-fledged dabbler—as disappointing. About the same percentage of men found disappointing a recent decision by some of the best singers in the chapter to leave it to form another chorus composed more exclusively of high-quality voices. Although there are men's and women's barbershop choruses in other cities that have experienced similar schisms and accompanying disappointment, this is hardly a routine occurrence. Nonetheless, tension lurks in many choruses between those who feel that anyone should be admitted who likes to sing and can carry a tune (this is the official policy of the three societies), and those who feel that their chorus should be composed strictly of singers who know their art well. All in all, however, disappointments are but a minor countersentiment to the high points that those in this study cherish mightily. The sweet in barbershop far outweighs the bitter.

ENDING THE CAREER

Since this study centered on currently involved barbershoppers, I have no systematic data on how their career comes to an end. Discussion with singers of both sexes suggests, however, that full examination of this matter will likely turn up at least four reasons for leaving: outside commitments, old age or death, loss of interest, and disenchantment. One can also drop out for a combination of these.

Outside commitments, such as those demanded by home and work, temporarily sidelined some of the respondents and prevented a number of others from participating to the extent they desired. Commitments of this sort can also remove a singer permanently from the barbershop scene, as in a transfer to another city.[4] Promotion to a more responsible and time-consuming position at work, pressure from children or a spouse to be at home more often, or a growing small business are among the typical outside commitments said in barbershop circles to pull some enthusiasts from the art for several years, even permanently.

Death as the reason for ending the career indicates that barbershop singers can and often do stay on well into old age. For some, the long hours on the risers become too painful or too exhausting, forcing them to accept an exclusive diet of service work or sit at the side of the chorus during rehearsals and performances. It is not unusual to see one or two elderly men or women situated, perhaps in wheelchairs, at one end of the risers as they and their chorus perform. Their voices are still good, but their physical condition demands special arrangements. Despite these accommodations, infirmity and immobility do eventually lead some singers to resign from the chapter as active members.

Disenchantment helps generate a loss of interest in barbershop and may indirectly enhance the appeal of another serious leisure field. Or it may simply push the singer out of barbershop to a sort of aimless casual leisure. Finally, it can result in a special partial abandonment, a shift to quartet singing only.

The disappointments mentioned earlier are not generally disenchanting. Rather, disenchantments spring from situations over which a barbershopper has little or no control, that create a sense of desperation the only apparent solution to which is to leave the chapter. Among the sources of disenchantment are cost, cliquishness, objectionable policy (e.g., tolerance of mediocrity, insistence on high standards), lack of leadership, weak or disliked choral directors, and preference for another style of unaccompanied, four-part harmony.

It appears that most barbershop chapters work hard to moderate the costs of this leisure, such as by fund-raising and ticket sales to their shows. Even then, chapter dues, trips to conventions, and uniforms and costumes exact a considerable sum from members, especially new ones. The latter must pay out a substantial initial amount toward the uniforms or costumes used by their chorus.

Preference for another style of unaccompanied, four-part harmony is one of the most prickly issues facing contemporary barbershop. The three barbershop societies exist to promote and, for the men, preserve barbershop song, an art form that has clear harmonic and structural roots in, among other forms, nineteenth century American popular music. Singers who want to sing music that is more dissonant, has a longer melody line, or is otherwise different from standard barbershop or who want to sing and entertain in such a way that they depart from that style, find themselves in conflict with the policies and goals of their society. One solution to this impasse is to leave the local chapter to join or establish a vocal ensemble more suitable to one's taste. This is certainly the end of the career in barbershop as that music is traditionally defined, but it is only a turning point in the serious leisure career of singing in general.

Conclusions

There is concern in all three barbershop societies about membership. In North America at least, membership growth has been alarmingly slower than general population growth. Moreover, there is a conspicuous absence of young adults, although, if our two samples are typical, this is somewhat truer for men's than for women's chapters. The mean age of the samples reflects this demographic fact: 45.6 for the women, 49.8 for the men, within age ranges of 25 to 75 and 32 to 75 respectively.[5] Nineteen percent or three of the women were below age thirty. There were no men in their twenties.

What remedies does this study suggest? In fact, only a few. Since most barbershop singers find their way into the art through friends and acquaintances, recruitment efforts should try to exploit these ties. Chapter members should talk to the men and women in their work, leisure, extended family, and especially their church choirs about the excitement they find in singing. For female singers, the high school glee clubs in their community may be an untapped source. A singout or two each year at different high schools (by quartets and choruses of both sexes) would give barbershop exposure where recruitment is weakest. One might also perform at nearby colleges and universities as well as try to gain a spot in local or even national television programs (television confers considerable prestige).

One of the oft-heard arguments in barbershop circles is that young adults are generally unattracted to barbershop because it is so different from the popular music that they and their peers enjoy. Yet, some later teenagers and young adults do take a substantial interest in other nonpopular forms of music, chiefly jazz and classical music. A proportion of these listeners even become vocal or instrumental performers of that music on an amateur or professional basis. Casual observation suggests further that these "unusual" musical interests are often sustained in parallel with peer group tastes in popular music. These segments of the young adult and late teenage population appear to be leading a quite comfortable dual musical existence. Is there any reason why a similar accommodation could not take place for some of the people in this age bracket with respect to barbershop?

It seems that, in their effort to preserve the traditional form, the barbershop societies are alienating the contemporary young adult (not to mention the disenchanted older adult) at a time in North American musical history when a wide gap has evolved between the nineteenth century popular music in which barbershop is based and the jazzlike, electronically-produced popular music of the 1980s and the 1990s. The fear in barbershop circles is that the old music will disappear if they let down their guard and allow in other forms of unaccompanied, four-part harmony. How realistic is this fear?

Let us return to jazz, which is also an original American music. When it began to evolve around approximately 1925 from what is known today as its traditional or dixieland form, there was no person or organization who successfully preserved it at that time. Yet traditional jazz ultimately regained its popularity, and is now considered one of several vibrant styles of the music.[6] The same historical pattern can be seen in classical music, one style of which even serves as the background for barbershop. For example, baroque, an early classical style, enjoys considerable popularity today. Innovations in jazz and classical music that fostered new styles were rarely lauded by the musical establishment of the day who were, for all that, powerless to stop their development. But all is well that ends well: there was resistance, and whereas the new styles eventually triumphed, they also failed to supplant the older ones.

But jazz and classical music were never and are still not nearly as organizationally controlled as modern barbershop. The three societies offer many indispensable services for the production of the art: coaching, printed music, financial support, opportunities for personal musical development, and artistic exposure (at contests, annual shows) all in the highly appealing atmosphere of camaraderie with other chapter members. Although not impossible, it is nonetheless difficult to do the barbershop of today without aid from one of the societies. They have, in short, a significant degree of monopoly control over the production of their music, and can thereby force members to accept their definition of what is acceptable barbershop. New styles cannot take root under these conditions.

In conclusion, the next move lies with the societies to loosen the reins somewhat. This might be done by holding contests for *free* as well as traditional barbershop.[7] The free form of quartet singing might be that of the Mills Brothers or, even more extreme, that of the Nylons or the black New Orleans group, Seduction.[8] The common ground between the two styles could be that both must be unaccompanied, four-part, vocal harmony that might even allow for the possibility of mixed sex units. It would be up to the societies to determine the specific ways of implementing this proposal such that those quartets and choruses that perform free barbershop would still have to do their share of preserving the traditional style. Indeed, Sweet Adelines International has already taken steps in this direction at its international convention.

Choruses and quartets may experiment in the performance package segment of the competition, an innovation made possible perhaps by the broader frame of reference of Harmony Inc. when compared with that of SPEBSQSA.[9] An opportunity to sing both styles might just be all that is necessary to attract some young adults and reattract some disenchanted members. What is needed at this point in the history of barbershop is an artistic safety valve, a role that free barbershop could possibly fill.

Notes

I am indebted to barbershop singers Don Clarke and Randy Peters for their careful and incisive comments on this chapter.

1. Someone who volunteers to do a largely unskilled task (e.g., take tickets, babysit) or give something (e.g., money, blood) is not a *career* volunteer as defined here.

2. This pattern may not hold up under survey sampling; barbershoppers themselves believe from their experiences that relatives are more important in this regard than the present study suggests.

3. Precise, unison pronounciation is crucial to the production of the rounded, ringing, consonant harmonies of traditional barbershop song. This effect is diminished or lost when, for instance, some singers pronounce "a" as "ah" and others pronounce it as "aw." It is also necessary, in order to achieve this sonority, that every singer start and stop the pronunciation and inflection of each syllable in each word at precisely the same time.

4. A transferred singer can also transfer his or her membership to the new local chapter, but heavy responsibilities in the new position and the probable absence of friends in the new chapter often turn out to be formidable barriers to overcome.

5. At fifty-five years, the mean age in SPEBSQSA is even higher (Report of the Select Committee on the Status and Future of the Society, 1988: 2).

6. The seemingly endless lines of people trying to enter Preservation Hall in New Orleans attest to the popularity of traditional jazz. Moreover, the Preservation Hall Band is in demand for concerts across North America.

7. Named after a similar arrangement in figure skating where there is also tension between innovation and tradition.

8. Seduction appeared briefly on CBS's "Super Bowl Saturday Night," 25 January 1990.

9. Harmony Inc. does not set for itself the goal of preservation of barbershop. Rather it is "a woman's organization dedicated to education and achievement through competition and performance of four-part harmony barbershop style" (*The Pitchpipe*, 1990: 16).

References

Knight, Mel, 1991. Personal communication (29 May).
Neulinger, John, 1981. *To leisure: An introduction.* Boston: Allyn and Bacon.

Pavalko, Ronald M. 1988. *Sociology of occupations and professions*, 2nd ed. Itasca, IL: F. E. Peacock.

Report of the Select Committee on the Status and Future of the Society. 1988. "A strategic plan for the barbershop harmony society." Kenosha, WI: SPEBSQSA.

SPEBSQSA. 1980. "Barbershop arranging manual." Kenosha, WI.

Stebbins, Robert A. 1970. "Career: The subjective approach." *Sociological Quarterly* 11:32–49.

———. 1979. *Amateurs: On the margin between work and leisure.* Beverly Hills, CA: Sage.

———. 1982. "Amateur and professional astronomers: A study of their interrelationships." *Urban Life* 10: 433–54.

———. 1984. *The magician: Career, culture, and social psychology in a variety art.* Toronto: Irwin.

———. 1992a. *Amateurs, Professionals, and Serious Leisure.* Montreal and Kingston: McGill-Queen's University Press.

———. 1992b. "Costs and rewards in barbershop singing." *Leisure Studies* 11:123–33.

The Pitchpipe. 1990. (January) 42: 16.

Van Til, J. 1979. "In search of volunt—ism." *Volunteer Administration* 12:8–20.

The Leisure Framework

PHILLIP BOSSERMAN

Introduction

The strum of an acoustic guitar or the close harmony of a barbershop quartet always beckon people to listen. Folk music has a persistent, universal appeal. Different forms of folk music have their periods of popularity and then wane, only to find revival. Such is the case with barbershop quartet singing. In the 1920s and 1930s this once very popular folk art declined to the point that it was very nearly extinct. Along came Owen C. Cash and Rupert I. Hall who enjoyed singing this style of music and knew there were others who felt the same way. They very innocently, and with utterly no idea a nationwide movement would emerge, invited some friends to meet on the roof garden of the Tulsa Club, Tulsa, Oklahoma, on April 11, 1938, to sing barbershop harmony. These twenty-six men had such a good time they decided to hold a second session a week later, and by their third meeting 150 men turned out at the Alvin Hotel to sing the old tunes in the patented barbershop close harmony style. The interest built. In a short time chapters sprang up all over the Midwest, ultimately stretching across the country. This folk music's revival continued, with its greatest growth after World War II.

Membership has declined since the start of the 1980s. Growth previously had been slow, approaching stagnation. The average age of the participants has increased, and fewer young men are entering the chapters' choruses and quartets. Is this the onset of another period of decline which this time may lead to barbershopping's extinction? Several reasons were advanced by the Society for the Preservation of Barber Shop Quartet Singing in America (SPEBSQSA) as to why barbershop singing declined after World War I: increasing urbanization, spread of the automobile, prohibition, the tempo of life becoming faster, radio provided music instantly, and "(popular) music itself was more dance-oriented, sophisticated, less vocally suitable and folksy."[1] At this juncture of the last decade of the 20th century, I want to describe the present context in which the changes within the organization are taking place.

I view the topics which follow as concentric circles representing the circuits of influence affecting barbershop singing as a hobby. The demographic profile of the United States population projected to 2050 is the first circle, then widening out to the circles of employment, mobility, and technological changes. These in turn lead to a consideration of the circle of time and how it is used by Americans, particularly noting the implication for free time and leisure. Then follow the circles of the physical environment, the distribution of wealth and power nationally and globally, ending with gender and ethnic relationships.

A Demographic Profile

Looking back we can see that the overwhelming reality of the post-World War II years was the incredible upsurge in births leading to a generational cohort of some 77 million strong. We have frequently called these children "the baby boomers." Taking the image of a pig in a python this cohort's bulge through the age structure has been particularly disruptive creating dislocations and painful adjustments every step of the way. The leading edge of that cohort (those born in 1944) is now forty-six years of age. All those born through the year 1964 are included in this generation. The decade 1950–1959 saw some 43 million babies born. That is 10 million more than the previous decade.

The total baby boom generation of 77 million represents nearly one-third of the present population. How did this baby boom generation happen? Besides the obvious answer that millions of couples made babies, it is not easy to determine why there was such a sudden and sustained increase over the span of a generation. More than a million Army wives were waiting for their spouses to come home after World War II and the result was what Landon Y. Jones calls "a massive affirmation of childbearing."[2] Marriages grew spectacularly as did divorces. And people married younger.

Three factors led to the resultant record rise in births: first, women who would have normally been having babies had to postpone bearing children until the war ended. They made up for lost time. Second, women were marrying at younger ages giving

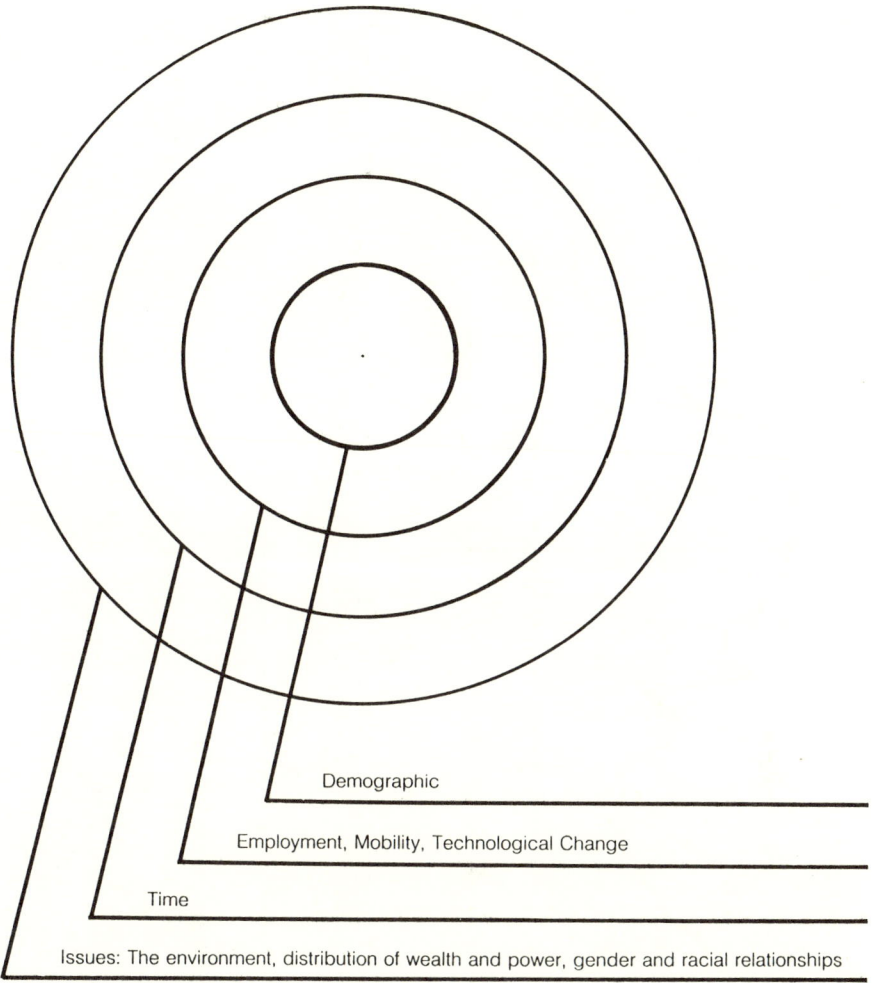

Figure 1

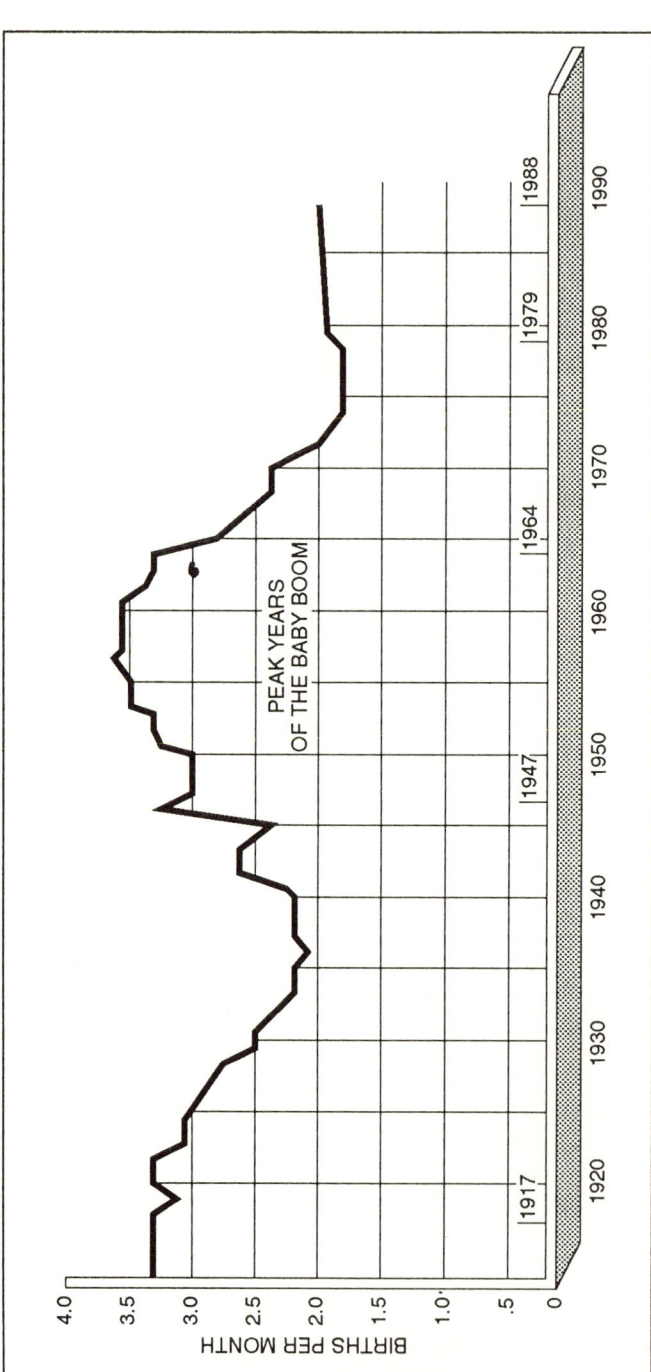

TABLE 1
Total Fertility Rates for U.S. Women: 1917–1987
SOURCES: 1917–75: Selma Taffel, *Trends in Fertility in the United States*, Vital and Health Statistics, Series 21: Data from the National Vital Statistics System, No. 28 (Hyattsville, Md.: National Center for Health Statistics, 1977), Table 13; 1976–77: U.S. Bureau of the Census, *Statistical Abstract of the United States, 1979*, Table 82; 1978: U.S. Bureau of the Census, "Population Profile of the United States: 1978," *Current Population Reports*, Series P-20, No. 336, Table 3; 1979: National Center for Health Statistic, Natality Division, personal communication, April 1980. Portion of figure pertaining to 1917–79 is reprinted form *Population Bulletin* 35, 1, p. 5, published by the Population Reference Bureau Washington, D.C.; National Center for Health Statistics, *Vital Statistics of the United States, Vol. 1—Natality* (Washington, D.C.: U.S. Government Printing Office, 1990). John E. Farley, *Sociology*, 2e, © 1992, p. 518. Reprinted by permission of Prentice Hall, Englewood Cliffs, New Jersey.

them additional years to bear children, and third, these women were having more children than the previous generation. Boom! The babies arrived in record numbers: in 1946, 3.4 million were born; 1947, 3.8 million more. "In 1946, the Census Bureau director said that the U.S. population would not reach 163 million until the year 2000."[e] Demographers were unimpressed with these first two years and even five years of record births. By 1953, the total U.S. population hit 160 million, thirty-seven years ahead of what they had projected.

Along with the Yanks coming home after the war and the enormous vitality of the new peacetime economy feeding the hungry households with durable goods, a procreation ethic hit the American culture with a bang contributing significantly to this baby boom generation. As stated above, two different groups of women were having babies, and lots of them: the wives of the GIs, catching up on years of separation, and the newly wedded at younger ages deciding to have more babies than previously expected. This latter group accounts for the sustained growth in births which lasted for a generation. A further explanation for such a population explosion is that these were mothers born in the 1930s who had a feeling of optimism about themselves and what their children could do. Their reasons for optimism are many. They were from the start nurtured by parents who were unburdened by lots of children. So they did not have to compete with many siblings for parental attention and resources. The same held true in schools, then later for jobs and careers. They were what one demographer has called "the Good Times Generation."[4]

The baby boom generation had an opposite experience. They competed at every turn for the attention of their parents, for resources, for spaces and good teaching in schools, for jobs and careers. Many have come up short with deep-seated longings, resentments, feelings of failure, and low self-esteem. As an answer to these feelings of frustrations and failure, there sprang up a plethora of new religious movements, psychotherapy techniques, groups, and ideas—some of which were bizarre and suspect. The Hare Krishnas, the Jonestown settlement which ended so tragically in mass suicidal deaths of hundreds, the Church of Scientology, satanic cults, the rites of the KKK, and the enormous growth of evangelicals are just a few examples.

Drawing upon the theoretical work of Talcott Parsons I would suggest that baby boomers have had an increased need for tension-management.[5] In order to accomplish this they have relied on the cultural experiences of religion and leisure, the latter expressed in recreation, artistic pursuits, socializing, television, travel and physical activity of all sorts. These baby boomers have been the trend setters in all these areas.

How have the barbershoppers been affected? Growth in this close harmony form of singing was most pronounced following World War II until the early 1950s. Then a serious decline in membership occurred falling from a high of 26,901 in mid-1950, to 22,609 in 1954. The Society made up most of this loss by 1957. The growth has been only about 10,000 since then. And as we have indicated, the average age of the participants is moving upward.

The pyramids in Table 2 show how the age structure of the United States population has fluctuated radically over the span of years from 1960 to the anticipated profile for the year 2040. The baby boom cohort is seen moving through the decades. The projected pyramids for 2000, 2020, and 2040 forecast a surge in the middle-age population with a startling increase in those over sixty-five. We can see well where the barbershoppers fit.

The barbershop singing hobby should have grown as the baby-boomers have aged but it has not in proportion to their number of the population. This is a crucial factor. There are several determinants at work here. Urbanization and suburbanization steadily continued, further separating the places where people live from where they work. The commute grew longer, adding work-related hours to each day and cutting into the time for rehearsals and performances. This may be changing as people increasingly work from their homes; or new kinds of business, including manufacturing, are more frequently locating in the suburbs.

Mobility increased in the post-World War II period and still remains high, with about 20 percent of the population moving each year. This has to have had an impact on barbershop quartet and chorus singing. However, there is a visible trend of increasing numbers of persons refusing to move. The actuality of more dual job and career households influences this mobility. If both spouses cannot find work at the same level as currently held, then one or the other will turn down the move even if it means finding other work, declining a promotion, or accepting some other limitation. This trend could be a positive development for barbershopping.

The conclusion we make is that this hobby did not keep up with the baby boomers as they moved through "the python." Real growth should be occurring. Why has it not? Do we return to the reasons given for the decline after World War I? Increasing urbanization, automobile use with longer commutes, drugs, a

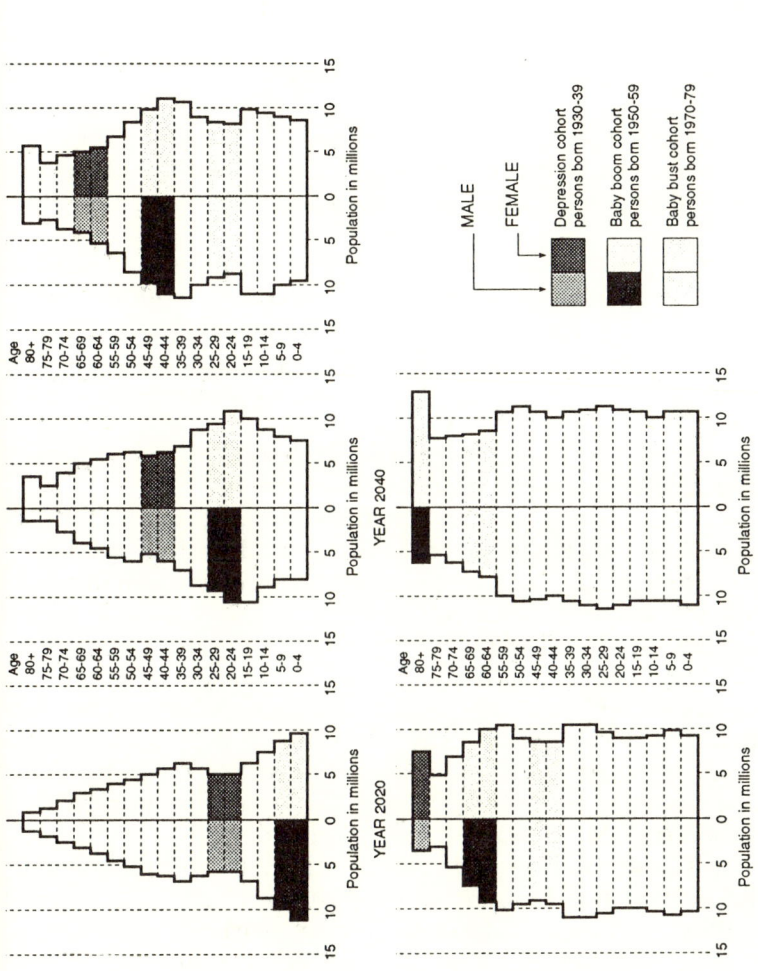

TABLE 2
Age-Sex Pyramids for the United States: 1960–2040

NOTE: 1980–2050 projections assume a total fertility rate rising to 2.0 births per woman by 1985 and constant thereafter; life expectancy at birth rising to 72.8 years for males and 82.9 years for females by 2050; net immigration constant at 750,000 persons per year.

SOURCES: 1960–70: U.S. Bureau of the Census, *1970 U.S. Census of Population: General Population Characteristics, United States Summary*, Vol. I, PC (1)-B1, 1972, Table 52; and 1980–2050: special unpublished tabulations prepared by Leon F. Bouvier for the Select Commission on Immigration and Refugee Policy, 1980. *Population Bulletin* 35, 1, p. 19. Reprinted by permission of the Population Reference Bureau, Washington, D.C.

faster-paced life, radio and television, and the nature of popular music itself which has been highly influenced by rock-and-roll making it inappropriate for close harmony singing? Are there other reasons brought on by the circumstances of today's world? We shall see.

Changing Types of Work

The nature and type of work have radically changed over the past twenty-five years with the transition to a service or information economy. The following chart shows just how dramatic this change has been.

Employment in the service sector of the economy (such activities as insurance, education, marketing, government, public relations, health delivery and the like) has a different quality to it. Most of this work is brain work. Very little physical labor is involved unless one is standing to deliver some kind of service, such as a clerk in a store.

The services use the technologies of the new electronics: computers, fax machines, copiers, graphics displays, and videos. Some key work-oriented concepts are planning, brainstorming, processing, modelling, integrating, synthesizing, and timing. A favorite tool is the flow chart. So work is often done in the form of a project and it is broken down into time intervals mapped on a flow chart indicating how long it will take to complete each project phase.

Usually workers will receive a salary rather than be paid by an hourly wage. They frequently receive bonuses if they complete a project on time or ahead of schedule. The office building has replaced the factory as the site where these service personnel work. The separation of home and employment is even more pronounced. These workers live in bedroom communities which encircle the city center. In their unending search for the single family dwelling in a desired bucolic setting, workers must commute ever longer distances to get to where the majority of the service agencies and establishments conduct their business. Time budget studies show that indeed they are taking longer to get to work each day.

As mentioned above, the new technologies do make it possible to stay at home and work in one's "electronic cottage." Alvin Toffler, who coined this phrase, notes that "[an] appreciable amount of work is . . . being done at home by such people as salesmen and

TABLE 3

Distribution of Work in the United States, 1947-1988

Primary Sector (In 1,000s of workers)	1947	% work force	1988	% work force
mining	952	1.8	721	.6
agriculture	7,891	15.2	3,259	2.9
Total	8,843	17.00	3,980	3.50
Secondary Sector (In 1,000s of workers)				
construction	1,982	3.8	5,125	4.5
manufacturing	15,942	30.7	19,406	17.1
Total	17,924	34.50	24,531.	21.60
Tertiary Sector (In 1,000s or workers)				
transportation and public utilities	4,166	8.0	5,548	4.9
trade	8,955	17.2	29,811	26.4
finance, insurance and real estate	1,754	3.3	6,677	5.9
services (business, personal, professional & entertainment)	5,050	9.7	24,971	22.1
government (includes those in uniquely governmental activities)	5,474	10.5	17,373	15.3
Total	25,399	48.70	84,380.	74.60
Total Work Force	51,772		112,907	

Source: Table No. 661,"Employment by Industry, 1970 to 1988, and Projects, 2000." _Statistical Abstract of the United States_. Washington, D.C.: Government Printing Office, 1991, and adapted from Seymour Wolfbein, _Work in American Society_. Glenview, Il: Scott, Foresman and Co., p. 34.

saleswomen who work by phone or visit, and only occasionally touch base at the office; by architects and designers; by a burgeoning pool of specialized consultants in many industries; by large numbers of human-service workers like therapists or psychologists; by music teachers and language instructors; by art dealers, investment counselors, insurance agents, lawyers, and academic researchers; and by many other categories of white-collar, technical and professional people."[6] Moreover, husband and wife partnerships are increasing, with self-employment on the rise.

All of these elements describe a very different way of life for employees in the service economy from that of the production worker. There is greater flexibility, larger periods of block time freed from work, job environments where informal discussions can take place because there is less noise. The ambience is different. Problem solving requires thinking time and group discussion. The dictates of the assembly line are much more muted, definitely in the background, though the ubiquitous in-tray and out-tray seem to resemble the unstoppable movement of the production belt.

We have already described how a tax attorney from Tulsa, Oklahoma and an investment banker in the same town "wrote a witty letter to friends inviting them to a song fest on the Roof Garden of the Tulsa Club, April 11, 1938."[7] This is how the barbershop singing organization got started. The founders were both service workers. No doubt the twenty-four others who appeared at the Tulsa Club that day also worked in the services. The point I'm making is that barbershoppers were and remain overwhelmingly men who work in the upper echelons of the service sector of the economy. (Barbers are service workers as far as that goes.) Serious barbershopper hobbyists are from the professional, technical, white-collar occupations implying that they usually will have postsecondary education degrees and enjoy incomes associated with these occupations.[8]

In sum, these factors of demography, type of employment, mobility, and technological changes are all a part of the context in which leisure, and more particularly barbershopping, takes place. Each person who sings in the choruses and quartets is buffeted by the winds of change these elements produce. An important structural feature which looms large in the contemporary context of barbershopping is time.

Time

Reports pour in about how Americans are hassled and hurried. They sense they have little time for themselves. They feel rushed.

They are what Steffan Linder called "the harried leisure class."[9] These types bring work home with them, get up early in order to be at the office before the main work force arrives, and often spend a good part of weekends pouring over reports, briefs, and writing memoranda. "Among 188 million people with full-time jobs last year (1989), nearly 24 percent—largely executive, professional, self-employed persons, journalists, bureaucrats, and the secretaries and clerks who toil alongside them—spent 48 or more hours a week on the job, according to the Bureau of Labor Statistics. Ten years ago only 18 percent worked so much."[10] Kilborn goes on, quoting Jerome Rossow, president of the Work in America Institute in Scarsdale, New York, "The leisure society in America is a myth." The work ethic seems to have become obsessive. "Part of the problem is that the salary increases continue to lag behind inflation, so workers have to run harder each year to stay even. At the same time, fewer people are entering the work force now that the baby boomers are grown up and employed; with fewer new workers for hire, companies try to squeeze more out of the ones they already have."[11] Does the economy gain from all this frenetic activity? The record is unclear.

What are some of the reasons people give for working longer and harder—harder because of the technological *wunderkind* like cellular telephones, fax machines, laptop computers, desktop computers with which to send electronic mail, and the like? "Most say they must to make ends meet. Some say they also relish the bustle. Some think that if they don't work harder the competition will. An executive at Chase Manhattan Bank said that when he stays on at the office and takes the 8:10 P.M. train home to Old Greenwich, or the 8:40 or the 9:10, 'I see a lot more Japanese. They're working late. You can't help but notice.'"[12] There are those who fear their own bosses and so work harder and longer. The eighties saw lots of middle-level jobs eliminated. Those who remain think they are vulnerable. Employers may be using more subtle means of squeezing out work. They make it easy for employees to buy home computers and some feel this is so they will do two or three hours of office work at home.

Some workers are experiencing ill health (high blood pressure and heart attacks, to mention just two) as a result of this stepped-up pace. Still the economy remains sluggish despite all of this intense activity. "We may be getting more throughput but no more output," notes Ronald E. Kutscher, associate commissioner of the Bureau of Labor Statistics.

This condition of frenetic bustle in the work force is sobering.

I have dwelt on this problem of time because barbershoppers overwhelmingly come from this group of people who are involved in longer work hours and more intense labor.

Hence, barbershoppers suffer from the perceived problem of a lack of time. The frequency with which persons drop out of choruses and quartets is very often tied to this sense that there is not enough time. Singing in this organization requries an enormous commitment of time. I must emphasize that the idea "there is not enough time" is a perception. Overall, free/leisure time has increased dramatically over the past 60 years. The long view corrects what perhaps is only a short-term cycle. Table 4 shows the decline in working hours in the United States over the past 130 years.

This table reports the average hours the work force as a whole labored over these decades. There were and still are those who stayed on the job much longer, as well as those who worked far fewer hours than the average. These extremes are smoothed over when reporting an average. Moreover, only about 67 percent of the adult work force over the age of eighteen works at a paid job on any given day.

Free/leisure time is a fact witnessed by the enormous presence of both public and private services delivering recreation and leisure to the population. Advertising attests to the high profile which leisure/free time has. Finally, whole lifestyles of the eighties and nineties, including serious leisure pursuits such as barbershopping, are built around hobbies, activities and interests which are separate entities from those related to employment in the formal economy. This free/leisure time is a social force, a powerful influence on our personal and collective behaviors.

Though these observations and statistics indicate that Americans have more rather than less free/leisure time—and this factor is influential in the social and personal lives of Americans—about 30 percent feel they are pushed for time. John Robinson, who conducts research on how people use their time through the method of personal diaries, concludes that "Americans have more free time at their disposal than they did twenty years ago, . . . they spend fewer hours working today then they did in 1965, and they are doing significantly less housework as well."[13] Yet they feel rushed, that is at least 30 percent do. A part of it is due to what we reported previously in that they feel they must work at their paid jobs harder and longer. However, another factor comes into play. People simply have more choices as to what they can do with their free time. They have consumed more in the way of equip-

Table 4

Average Weekly Hours Per Worker,
Civilian Economy, Selected Years, 1869-1990

Years	National Bureau of Economic Research	Bureau of Labor Statistics
1868-78	53.2	
1879-88	53.4	
1890	53.7	
1900	53.2	
1910	52.1	
1920	49.8	
1930	47.7	
1940	43.9	
1943	46.6	48.5
1944	47.0	47.8
1945	45.7	46.1
1946	43.5	44.3
1947	42.4	43.5
1948	42.0	42.8
1949	41.6	42.1
1950	41.2	41.7
1951	41.0	42.2
1952	41.0	42.4
1953	41.0	41.9
1954	40.5	40.9
1955		41.6
1956		41.5
1957		41.0
1958		40.6
1959		40.5
1960		40.5
1961		40.5
1962		40.5
1963		40.4
1964		40.0
1965		40.5
1966		40.4
1967		40.4
1968		40.1
1969		39.9
1970		39.1
1975		38.7
1980		36.6
1986		35.1
1990		34.5

Source: For 1869-1970 dates see Hedges, Janice and Moore, Geoffrey, "Trends in Labor and Leisure," Monthly Labor Review, Feb. 1971, Table 1. For 1970-75 data see Employment and Earnings, Table 22, Jan. 1976; for 1976-1990 data see Monthly Labor Review, May, 1991 and April 1989, Employment and Earnings, Table 12.

ment for recreational and leisure use: fishing tackle, a boat, camper, tennis racquet, bowling ball, video camera and player, CD player, jogging gear, backpacking paraphernalia, a bicycle, ad infinitum. It takes time to use these accessories and care for them. Additionally, think of the heavily advertised possibilities to use this free/leisure time: time sharing in a condo in Hawaii, season tickets to the symphony or theater, membership in the local country club which includes a golf course, tennis court, swimming pool, and dining room where part of the membership requirement is to eat in the dining room at least three times a month. The list is endless. No wonder, then, that a person feels incredibly rushed. How can I possibly do even a fraction of these things? And then there is barbershop quartet practice and singing with the chorus along side of these other competing claims on my time. An African poem seems to say it all:

SONG OF AN UNLUCKY MAN[14]

Chaff is in my eye,
A crocodile has me by the leg,
A goat is in the garden,
A porcupine is cooking in the pot,
Meal is drying on the pounding rock,
The King has summoned me to court,
And I must go to the funeral of my mother-in-law:
In short, I am busy.

Robinson points out some interesting habits of these persons who report "always" feeling rushed. "[They] work more hours per week than the average person, and they spend more time caring for children as well—particularly chauffeuring them around. But they do no more housework than the average person. They spend less time grocery shopping than those who feel less rushed, but spend about the same amount of time shopping for clothes and other products . . . they spend more time taking care of themselves—washing and grooming—than the average persons. They spend less time eating than the average, particularly meals at home. They also spend less time sleeping at night, and they take fewer naps as well. . . . they spend more time involved in organizational activities—with the exception of attending church services. They spend more time in active sports and attending sports events. They also spend more time talking to people, both face-to-face and on the telephone. But they spend less time reading or writing letters than those who feel less busy. [Finally], they watch less television, almost 30 percent less. They spend less time visiting friends and relatives, going to parties, working on hobbies and just doing nothing."[15]

Robinson's portrait of those 30 percent who feel they are squeezed for the time to do what they need or want to do, I would conjecture, fit the socioeconomic level of many of those who are members of the barbershop organization. Why do some of these 30 percent choose to sing the close harmony, barbershop style? Why do they commit themselves to the quantity of time it takes them to attend practices and perform? Other members of this research team are seeking to answer these questions. A question that arises in the face of these observations is why barbershopping does not have a stronger appeal among the other socio-economic levels?

Beyond the Other-Directed Person

David Riesman in his celebrated study, *The Lonely Crowd*,[16] sees a link between population shifts, their growth and decline and social character. He sees the other-directed type of personality develop in a society where the population is in decline and its members are aging. Other people become the problem. Relationships are all important. "You're OK, I'm OK" becomes the litmus test. An old joke sums it up: How do two psychiatrists greet each other on the street? The first says, "You're fine, how am I?"

However, this runs into a contradiction with the current situation in America brought on by that huge age cohort, the baby boomers. Presently, births are in decline after the explosive record number of new babies during the late forties, fifties, and early sixties. Now a "psychology of scarcity" has set in among employers, in particular, who expect the same amount of work out of a smaller work force. Add into the mix the workers we described above who are professional, self-employed, and the like. They agree with the employers and often are compelled by the inner-directed ethnic which characterized those independent, hard-driving entrepreneurial types of the 18th and 19th centuries when the death rate began to decline in industrializing America. Yet they are an anomaly, a contradiction, in that we live in this postmodern, postindustrial era where the dominant character mode and social ethic is that of *other-direction*. What I find surfacing here is an unexpected outcome of Riesman's description:

"The psychology of abundance," an attribute of the postindustrial era we supposedly are in, has turned towards a "psychology of scarcity." The more we have translates into less. Our possession of things is insatiable and the economy encourages this at every turn. In fact, planned obsolescence is necessary for an economy based on growth and consumption. We constantly receive signals that our expected role is that of worker, i.e., producer, provider, maker, server, but the real task is consumer. Many assure us we are entering the free/leisure time society, but again, the psychology of scarcity obtains. We *think* we do not have the time to do what we want. Yet all the indices point to a *real* growth in freed time from paid work. What this seems to say is that we have little understanding of what leisure can mean: solitude, contemplation, conviviality, sharing in a task whether it be making music, a garden, building a house together, planning and then putting on some event like a peace fair, or an arts festival or a block party.

The above discussion on this important structural dimension of time has turned on an effort to explain why we have this feeling of "time famine,"[17] or why we are not motivated to choose certain kinds of activities because free time seemingly is scarce. A final reason why this might be so has to do with paid employment itself. The social science literature is overwhelming in its conclusions that job satisfaction is lacking for upwards of 80 percent of all workers in this modern, industrial economy. The 20 to 30 percent who do find gratification in the paid work they do come once again from that upper socioeconomic tier we mentioned earlier. Such a high incidence of job dissatisfaction and frustration is a devastating condemnation of the present economic order in and of itself. The one area where workers do agree there is a measure of satisfaction is that of interpersonal contact with office colleagues or factory friends. But the job itself has no intrinsic worth. It is strictly a means to an end, that end being what they want to do with their free time, especially leisure. What does a debilitating, demeaning job do to a person's spirit, a job where one is not valued for what she thinks, or has a voice in the decisions affecting performance, workplace environment and organization? The answer is clear: such a condition kills the spirit. Such workers naturally seek escape from six, seven, eight hours or longer on a job doing what really seems of little use now or in the long run. The time budget studies bear out how they overwhelmingly escape this trapped, untenable condition: television. This is by far the leisure activity of choice. (Is it really a choice?) Nearly all the time gained from paid work over the past twenty years has been turned into time looking at television whether it be programming or video films. And the surprising, even alarming thing, is that it makes no difference what the educational level is! All persons have put this additional free time into watching the tube.

The outcome is that when a person is asked if he has time to do this activity or that, often he responds with an emphatic "NO!" Television is part of his everyday life, an ironic necessity like the automobile, which means that for many there is not enough time to join a service club, share in organizing a recycling program, making a garden, or pursuing a serious hobby like barbershopping. The TV is on for an average of more than seven hours a day in American homes.

Wider Circles

I have thus far described several of the concentric circles which form the context of United States citizens. I have done this by looking at the nature of the population as a whole and what is happening to it, including the influence of significant past events and the possible shape of this population in the future. Secondly, I examined the way we are employed and the changing patterns of paid jobs. This led to a consideration of time and how it is allocated between work and non-work which includes free time and leisure time. Though free/leisure time has increased over the past four decades, some 30 percent of the work force feel constantly rushed; they experience a kind of "time famine." Implied in this discussion is that every social institution—the family, schools and colleges, religion, polity, and the economy itself—is affected by these dynamics, producing within them dislocations, contradictions and tensions.

Other, ever-widening circles complete this context. First is the environmental crisis which more and more people at the grassroots are sensing is a serious problem we can no longer safely ignore. The multiple threats of pollution, waste, high energy consumption, and commitment to growth at any cost (where bigger is always better) are ripping gaping holes in the ozone layer and creating the specter of the globe heating up at an alarming rate. In a few decades the polar ice caps will melt, causing the waters to rise and posing serious threats to seaboard lands of Florida and the eastern shore of Maryland. The changes in the weather patterns these conditions will produce will profoundly affect agriculture and threaten one of the world's biggest bread baskets, the central plains of the United States. Other agricultural areas worldwide will likewise feel the impact of the global weather changes. We live on a fragile spaceship which is feeling the whiplashes of an industrial world economy that knows no limits. The affluent populations of the Northern tier, "developed," countries particularly are consuming at high, bordering on obscene, levels. Their consumption alone is fueling the fires heating up the globe.

A second, ever-widening concentric circle is that of Third and Fourth World poverty. The countries of the South, which make up nearly three quarters of the world's population, are left with only 20 to 25 percent of the world's goods, services and energy to use. This disparity is growing. The gap is expanding between the rich and the poor nations. Such inequality breeds poverty, violence, political instability, racism, rampant population growth, and enormous dislocations of people. We see this today in the Sudan and Ethiopia. Add to this deep-seated longings by particular ethnic groups to have their independence from powerful, politically entrenched majorities. These yearnings account for many of the wars currently ravaging countries such as Ireland, El Salvador, Sri Lanka, Ethiopia, Chad, the Philippines and Angola. Just as we cannot ignore the environmental crisis, so this acute inequality among nations has to be faced by the United States. The only way this can have meaning is if it becomes an issue at the grassroots.

This same inequality becomes more intrusive in our lives here in the United States as we gather the latest statistics on what is happening to this democratic society. The middle class is shrinking at an alarming rate. Five percent of the nation's households receive more income than the 30 percent at the bottom. One in every four children now lives in poverty. What kind of a future does this signal? The United States' society reflects increasingly the disparity among the world's nations. The gap between the rich and the poor is widening at such an alarming rate that we are creating two societies, something so feared by this nation during the terrible race riots of the late 1960s. What progress was made then in response to the burning of so many center cities has been wiped out. In short, the situation has become worse.

The visit of Nelson Mandela to the United States in 1990 contributed greatly to an expanding realization of the indispensable necessity to confront the problem of racism. This scourge is worldwide. When we realize that the population of the South (the southern tier of nations which are in the Third and Fourth Worlds) is predominantly people of color, and that the North (the northern tier of countries which make up the developed world) is populated overwhelmingly by Caucasians, we begin to understand how racism becomes an integral part of the relations among peoples of different nations and within these nations. Race and economic status are often linked together, resulting in the inference that technological and economic superiority is due to race. Of course this false linkage has little if anything to do with it when we realize that the most formidable economic power today is that of Japan, whose people have yellow skins. Again, this global plague of racism has infected the relations of people within American society. The rise of racial incidents and increase in minority group discrimination during the decade of the eighties make us painfully aware that Martin Luther King's dream of a society where brotherhood and sisterhood prevail is a long way from being realized.

Such circles of crisis in the world call attention to how important it is for everyone to recognize these realities. The arts have had a long history of social criticism. They have served in part as a conscience for whole groups of people. Folk art is no exception. Recall that during the 1950s, 1960s and early 1970s the medium of folk music carried the basic themes so important to the social movements of those revolutionary years. Max Kaplan notes that

> [T]he functions of the arts emerge as various needs arise.... The overlapping of the social and aesthetic was illustrated more recently during the bombing of Lebanon. According to the *New York Times* of 13 May 1982, while the Israelis and the PLO were engaged in sharp exchanges, a two-day art fair in West Beirut attracted four hundred thousand persons. Its organizer, George Zenny, remarked, "We are experiencing an inflation of creativity. At the same time, six theatrical productions were being held in the war-torn city, about 10 different art exhibitions were open, and both radio and TV were regularly presenting popular entertainment."
>
> Mr. Charles Rizk, the head of Lebanon's public TV system, observed in the *Times* article, "When simply walking down the street becomes a matter of life and death, people start to ask themselves very fundamental questions. And what is cultural if not expressions of man's questioning himself about his ultimate destiny?"[18]

This is certainly where we are in the midst of these whirling circles of crisis. They often seem out of control. The need is here, near. The arts have a role to play; indeed, they are the bellwether, the third eye for society and can contribute to both consciousness raising and pointing us in the direction we must go if we are to survive. That is what is at stake.

The barbershoppers have a part to play in all of this. There are signs that they are taking the lead in confronting some of these issues.

Conclusions

I have sought to describe the present context in which SPEBSQSA finds itself. Let me summarize the elements making up this social and cultural context and the implications for the organization. First, the demographic profile shows us a society which is generally aging. SPEBSQSA reflects the "greying" of the nation. However, we noted that the organization did not recruit as many new members from the baby boom generation as the size of that generation warranted. This perhaps is the critical factor which has contributed to membership decline. On the other hand, as these baby boomers age they may be more ready to join in singing the "old songs." I would suggest then that an effort might be made to recruit from this aging, baby boom generation pool.

Second, the socioeconomic level of those who are members of barbershop choruses and quartets reflects the occupations in the service sector of the economy. This means that barbershopping draws mostly from the middle class to upper middle class. What about their appeal to other socioeconomic levels? And we might note particularly the lack of participation by minorities such as blacks and hispanics. Are all of these potential fields of recruitment?

Third, we discussed the structural feature of time. Barbershoppers tend to be in service sector occupations and this means that they would be among those who sense a "time famine;" they feel pressed for time to do the things they have to do and they want to do. This sense of being rushed and harried is not due to a declining amount of time from paid work. On the contrary, this free time has steadily increased over the past fifty years. The growth in the cultural base has complicated life enormously and added to our consciousness of the seemingly countless numbers of things beckoning us to try and experience. The exponential growth in material goods like sports equipment, and outlets for cultural expression have caused us to feel we do not have time. "Stop the world, I want to get off!" may be a cry of many of us. Barbershopping is just one of the many activities competing for people's time. Fatigue and overload set in. Moreover, we noted that the kind of jobs the vast majority have bring little satisfaction.

Time budget studies indicate that for the population as a whole, the time gained from paid work over the past twenty years has been translated into watching television. It is the great escape. Perhaps local chapters would benefit from doing a modified time budget study of their members to see just how they spend their time. An examination of scheduling for practices, concerts, competitions and the like might be important. Does the competitive structure itself create the sense of being hassled, a feeling of necessity and constraint which contributes to a kind of leisure activity which reflects the work world one is seeking to forget or at least counterbalance? Are not work and leisure opposite poles of a continuum? If work becomes leisure and leisure work, then the distinctiveness of each will have disappeared, rendering them meaningless.

Fourth, the wider circles of this social and environmental context in which Americans live point to critical issues they must address. The arts are a medium by which this is done. I would suggest that SPEBSQSA consider changing their policy about the content of the songs they sing and/or link their singing to supporting a movement for the amelioration of one of the problems mentioned above rather than primarily being committed to Chamber of Commerce-like activities such as helping to open a new mall which promotes more consumerism, a definite factor contributing to the environmental crisis we face. In the Tucson winter meeting, 1990, Sweden's Sweet Adeline's International Champion Quartet and one of the American champion male quartets sang together the very moving song "Let There Be Peace on Earth and Let It Begin with Me." That is the type of content I mean.

Recently, National Public Radio featured a ninety-year old retired physician who sings in a barbershop quartet in Oregon. The quartet entertains audiences who come to hear them, but the quartet has another agenda—to teach these listeners how to maintain healthy bodies. This doctor featured on NPR not only sings in a barbershop quartet but is also a marathon runner and holds the records for that distance for several different age levels. He only started running when he was sixty!

This same kind of thing could be done for "housing for all," "health care for everyone," "let there be peace in the world," "think globally, act locally," "stop global warming," and "we are the world." The barbershop craft of a cappella four-part harmony is a genuine American-grown tradition. It could literally help keep America alive while preserving this distinct form of music.

If the organization wishes to appeal to the baby boomers and to youth, then this kind of adaptation is required. To paraphrase Charles Rizk, "What is barbershopping as a part of culture if not an expression of human questions about ultimate destiny?" This has to be the centerpiece of what we are doing. It does not have to be all there is to it. Entertainment and festivity are crucial to a culture as well. But by giving barbershopping a depth and breadth, I am convinced its appeal will expand. And we'll all be better for it.

Notes

1. *Information Manual for the Barbershop Quartet.* Kenosha, WI: SPEBSQSA, 1987, p. 3.
2. Landon Y. Jones, *Great Expectation.* New York: Ballentine Books, 1980, p. 10.
3. *Ibid.,* p. 11.
4. Attributed to Carl Hater of Tulane by Landon Y. Jones, *Ibid.,* p. 20.
5. See Phillip Bosserman, "The Division of Labor and Leisure in Modern Society: A New Form of Solidarity," in *Loisir et societe/Society and Leisure,* Vol. 3, No. 1.
6. Alvin Toffler, *The Third Wave.* New York: William Morrow and Co. Inc., 1980, 213.
7. Joe Liles, *Information Manual for the Barbershop Quartet.* Kenosha, WI: SPEBSQSA, 1987, p. 3.
8. See Robert Stebbins' chapter, "Becoming A Barbershop Singer," for a breakdown of occupations of some members of the Society for the Preservation and Encouragement of Barbershop Singing in America.
9. Steffan Linder, *The Harried Leisure Class.* New York: Columbia University Press, 1970.
10. Peter T. Kilborn, "Tales From the Digital Treadmill," *The New York Times,* June, 1990, Section 4.
11. *Ibid.*
12. *Ibid.*
13. John P. Robinson, "Time Squeeze," in *American Demographics,* Feb., 1990, p. 30.
14. Leonard W. Doob, editor, *A Crocodile Has Me By the Leg.* New York: Walker and Company, 1967.
15. *Ibid.,* pp. 32–33. The *Utne Reader,* No. 46, July/August, 1991, devotes its cover story to the theme, "For **Love** or **Money:** Making a Living vs. Making a Life." Several articles in this section treat such issues as: how to make a living without shortening their lives, the ups and down of deliberately deciding to get out of the fast lane, something is drastically wrong with the American workplace, and the increasing number of social problems attributable to overwork. Solutions: reduce work time and change how we work.
16. David Riesman with Nathan Glazer and Reuel Denney, *The Lonely Crowd.* New Haven: Yale University Press, 1961.
17. Geoffrey Godbey, "Anti-Leisure and Public Recreation" in Stanley Parker, et al, *Sport and Leisure in Contemporary Society, London: London, Polytechnic of Central London, 1975, p. 47.*
18. Max Kaplan, *The Arts: A Social Perspective.* Rutherford, N.J.: Fairleigh Dickinson University Press, 1990, p. 28.

Barbershoppers and Music Educators: Elitist/Populist Dualisms and the American Music Preservation Problem

J. TERRY GATES

As a music educator working with barbershoppers, I was surprised at the depth of concern for acceptance that I found in these skilled and dedicated men. It sounded familiar. Music educators and women barbershoppers are equally concerned. This concern for acceptance seems driven by a few "engines"—musical, social, cultural, and, of course, economic. My surprise at its depth provided the impetus for this paper.

The practical need for economic support and the universal desire for status would easily explain this concern if barbershopping's leaders did not frequently couple it with a desire for entree into the American music education establishment. Economic support (future members) or preservation might explain this desire, also. However, the leadership is dominated by skilled and dedicated barbershoppers who are also successful businessmen (and -women), public servants, and professionals. Such people use much more direct and measurable means to get new customers or users, develop customer loyalty, and broaden the circle of public acceptance for their establishments. There is more to this hoped-for connection with music education than mere economics, however.

The purpose of this essay is to explore the relationship between barbershopping and the music education establishment in America. I will use the term "music education" here in its narrow, institutional sense: the transmission of musical skills, knowledge, and values in public, private, and parochial schools by licensed or otherwise-credentialed music teachers. Music education in its broader sense (the sense I prefer and normally use) has a cultural rather than a societal base: the "perpetuat[ion of] a culture's musical skills, knowledge, and values by causing following generations to learn them." (Gates, 1990a, 31–32) Music educators, barbershoppers, symphony managers, shape-note singers—all are part of this culture-based music education activity, some more intensely than others. It is music education in the narrower, institutional sense, however, that concerns barbershoppers. I will use this narrower sense of the term in this paper. Because this paper is written about the Society for the Preservation and Encouragement of Barber Shop Quartet Singing in America, the term "barbershopper" will refer to male barbershop music singers. My preliminary studies of female barbershoppers, however, reveal that the two groups have nearly identical concerns.

My use of the dualism "elitist/populist" in this paper's title reveals something of the way this exploration will proceed. "Elitism" and "populism" are value systems that operate in any stratified society. For this paper, the stereotypically elitist tendencies of those Americans associated with art music and the populist tendencies of those associated with commercial and sentimental music are intended pairings, made with the full awareness that these stereotypes may be distasteful to some. Warner's seminal work (1949), however, gave stereotypes such as these some empirical basis. Espousing or reflecting elitist or populist values affects economic support. A particular cultural institution finds that support comes relatively easily if the institution's activities resonate with the social values of the stratum of the society that supports it. As I will point out below, music educators' goals and activities have an unclear, equivocal relationship with elite and populist traditions. This explains somewhat the persistently precarious position that music education has "enjoyed" in American schools for the last century and a half. Barbershoppers' musical and entertainment values align rather clearly with populist values.

MUSICAL ELITISM IN AMERICA

Kaplan's insightful summary of the history of arts education (1990, ch. 15–17) tells enough of the interplay between high art and crafts, between artist and artisan, to suggest that the dichotomy outlined above is relatively new in Western civilization. Both Levine (1988) and Blair (1988) placed the onset of the musical aspects of the elitist-populist dualism in America at about 1900, around the time of barbershop music's reputed roots. Blair finds the American elitist-populist dualism grounded and nourished by the distinctively different social structures that became attached by tradition to various European cultural pursuits. Levine (and Small, 1987) found the dualism rooted in American industrial-society values. Levine chronicles the "taming" of the American audience by high-culture concert managers and art gallery directors, actions prompted by their high-society patrons. His view is that the common citizen began to resent these attempts to "gentrify" arts consumers and began to avoid high-arts events, a type of boycott that nineteenth century Americans (and Elizabethan-era "groundlings") would not have found necessary. American artistic elitism, then, began about a century ago and was caused, according to Levine, by the demand for homogeneity in audiences from those wealthy patrons who supported artistic institutions. Blair concluded that the demand for homogeneity was transferred from European high culture. Regardless of its source, the effect was to separate the general populace from high art, a separation that people such as Walter Damrosch, Theodore Thomas, Leonard Bernstein, and most music educators have worked since then to eliminate.

It is equally possible that the artists and musicians brought this separation on themselves. Salmen (1983) notes that nineteenth century European musical artists fostered in their entourage (including their students) the bigoted notion that they constituted a kind of priesthood, with capacities to which lesser musicians could not aspire. Managers of cultural institutions reinforced these notions by taming the noisily participative behavior of the audiences in concert halls and art museums (Levine, 1988). These phenomena persist today—the bigotry of some musicians' entourages, the socioeconomic stratification expressed in cultural traditions and institutions, and the expectation that audiences would behave differently in the presence of high art and low art. These phenomena affect the value systems—the hopes, goals, measures of success—and, therefore, the behavior of barbershoppers and music educators alike.

The highbrow/lowbrow dualism in American music education, however, predates its emergence in the rest of society by nearly two centuries. The dualism was well established in New England as early as 1720, when Cotton Mather and others insisted that congregational singing needed immediate improvement. Their remedy was universal music literacy and their preferred strategy was the church-based singing school. The singing school, valued as much for its social as its educational benefits, had elitist purposes: music literacy and accurate, chorus-type singing. (Temperley, 1981; Gates, 1990b) The best and most loftily motivated of the singing schools' students, however, formed or joined choral societies. This provided the foundation for a dual system of music instruction, one in singing schools (and private studios) and one in choral societies, both of them elitist. Populist music instruction in parlors and on front porches continued although its vitality, then as today, is hard to document. "The masses have no history."

By the early 1800s, both singing schools and choral societies were well established. Singing schools achieve music literacy by the use of either standard or unconventional notations; high-art choral societies admit members with the understanding that they would be expected to read standard musical notation. Pedagogies diverged subtly by 1800. William Billings's rough-hewn advice for music teaching in America's Revolutionary War period was practical and full of tips for keeping students' noses to the grindstone. Lowell Mason's advice for teachers of the middle nineteenth century, based on his work in Boston's Academy of Music, and on the work of Swiss pedagogue Johann Pestalozzi, prescribed content and method in more polite, elitist terms. Lowell Mason and his supporters convinced the Boston School Committee of 1837 to fund vocal music instruction in grammar schools patterned after Mason's elitist model (song singing and music reading instruction). After an experimental start in Boston, Mason's Boston Academy model for vocal music instruction spread through the emerging American cities' school systems. Singing schools retreated to the rural regions, where events such as these were valued for their social benefits as much as for their educational efficiency. Today, singing schools are associated primarily with the shape-note traditions in America's "Bible Belt." Analyses of current shape-note singing practices by Mai Hogan Kelton, Buell Cobb, Hugh McGraw, James Scholten and others reveal that this tradition retains the elitist purposes of early eighteenth century reformers of psalmody, albeit in populist social settings.

The distinction between high culture and popular culture is easier to recognize than to describe, because culture is a dynamic process rather than a static one. Although many have attempted to explain it, I will not review these many theories here. The approach I will use is to recognize tendencies—predispositions evidenced by stereotypical, even archetypal, elitist and populist behavior. In his response to a point of view on elitism in music, Haack (1987, p. 20) catalogs some leading elitist and populist tendencies:

Elitist tendencies	*Populist tendencies*
Experts have the best knowledge of what is good music	Good music is what people find best meets their legitimate needs

Barbershoppers and Music Educators

Objective: focus out on the music	Subjective: focus in on persons
Art for art's sake	Art for people's sake
"Aesthetic" orientation	"Functional" orientation
What music people should use	What people should use music for
Measure it; study it	Feel it; experience it
Formalist, intellectual, contemplative, institutional, etc.	Expressionist, emotional, sensual, individual, etc.
Which is good (all types and styles judged on same basis)	Which music is good for what (types and styles judged on their own basis)
Excellence in terms of general absolutes: an excellent piece of music is good whether it is a funeral dirge or a wedding march	Excellence in terms of what kind, for whom, when, and where: a good funeral dirge makes a poor wedding march

Although this list has some room for argument its dichotomies are clear enough for illustration. To this list I would add some elitist and populist music performance tendencies that have educational implications:

Acoustical characteristics of the natural instruments (including the voice) govern performances	Electronic means of sound enhancement are expected parts of the presentation
Ensembles use printed music	Ensembles use memorized music
Personal performance repertoire is expanded through reading new music	Personal repertoire is expanded through rote learning new music
Skilled sight-reading reduces need for repetition	Repetition is standard method of learning new music
Conscious avoidance of dance-like movement by musicians in concerts	Movement is choreographed or, at least, expected in presentations
Auditorium-stype presentation: performers and attentive audience face each other	Conversation-style presentation: performers often face other performers; participative audience circles performers when physical conditions permit

This list is incomplete, and a whole catalog of tonal and rhythmic dichotomies could be added, starting with from observations such as this: it is unlikely that the Chicago Symphony Chorus would record an album of barbershop music unless they were willing to duplicate the sound of a barbershop chorus.

Within each of these cultural streams there are educational tendencies that display themselves in the behavior of teachers and learners:

Expert analysts, historians, and critics provide content	Expert performers and producers provide content
Emphasis on independent musicianship: it is a set of competencies that can be applied by any music	Emphasis is on skilled, memorized performance of specific musical examples
Teachers are credentialed by an elite institution, or by demonstrated success within elite institutions (concert stage, etc.)	Teachers are credentialed individually by students—"I will learn from you if I decide you have something to teach me."

In several important respects, both elitist and populist music traditions are similar in their educational tendencies:

Reinforced imitation of a skilled model is the basic pedagogy, especially of performance skills and values.

The teacher-learner dyad explains the relationship of pre-adults

and the roles of ensemble members of all ages with respect to the percentage of elapsed time devoted to the activity or preparing a piece of music for performance. (In quartets the person who expresses an idea for improving the product is, for that moment, the "teacher.")

In several respects, elitist and populist musical performance values also converge:

Public presentations should be well rehearsed

There is a leader whose prior study of the music to be performed establishes his/her prima facie claim to leader status

Performers should attain enough control over the pitch, timbre, loudness, and duration of tones to use these acoustical features of sound expressively

All of these matters have implications for the teaching and learning that goes on in rehearsals of all kinds: symphony orchestras, barbershop choruses and quartets, elementary school bands as well as bluegrass bands. In groups associated most strongly either with elitist or populist traditions, violating the value system of the tradition meets with little support. Insisting that a barbershop chorus read music, or teaching a symphony orchestra its parts by rote, would not earn the person who tried it as leader a permanent place in his or her role.

Today's music educator borrows freely from both elitist and populist traditions. The school choral conductor is traditionally expected to be an expert pianist and voice teacher as well as a musical leader. These characteristics mirror the traditional (elitist) opera coach's competencies. Today, however, high school choral directors and many church choir leaders use tape-recorded accompaniments by pianists and other musicians, most of them commercially produced, a populist expedient. Electronic synthesizers, drum sets, electric guitars and basses, and amplified singers' sounds (populist tendencies) have a firm place in churches of many denominations. Not long ago they were banned. The thoroughly elitist choral director does not use these enhancements; the thoroughly populist choral director would not be without them. The music educator uses them selectively to meet specific needs of musical style or practicality. Generations of choral teachers have attempted to teach Americans to read music. This attempt continues, but weakly. The elitist values that animated the attempt are losing in influence after literally centuries of promoting them. Among vocal musicians today (and many types of instrumentalists) advanced sight singing abilities are treated as useful skills but subordinate to control over pitch, tone quality, rhythm, and dynamics. Music educators have generally adopted the view that performance quality must take precedence over literacy when a choice must be made.

Music educators to whom I have shown the lists of elitist and populist tendencies above report that their teaching activities borrow from both lists, depending upon the circumstances in which the skills are needed. Most other musicians (the Chicago Symphony Chorus, for example, or a Cajun band) would choose as descriptive a greater percentage of the statements on one side or the other of the lists above. Their responses would be more unified than those of educators. The reason for the difference is important: Traditionally, performers attempted to be clear about what type of audience they wished to draw, elitist or populist. Most early music educators, on the other hand, felt mission-bound to emphasize those important musical values that were presumed to be missing in their students' own surroundings. They assumed uncritically that what was missing were elitist musical activities and tried to plug the gap: teach music reading, take student groups to high-art concerts, attend concerts of local town bands or visiting bands that contained many transcriptions of symphonic music, teach the plots of famous operas, form classes of children into choruses and give "concerts" at parents' meetings, etc. Music educators who acted on these beliefs had the clear mission to promote elitist musical values. Because of this, there was clarity in the relationships among their mission, the stratum of their societal support for this mission, and their methods of fulfilling it.

Contemporary music educators, however, take a broader view and this causes them some trouble. Music educators feel responsible for connecting the young with the musical life of their society—as many levels of it as possible. If one takes this responsibility seriously, then one draws freely from *both* sides of the lists above without assuming that students' out-of-school situations are dominated by either elitist or populist tendencies. Music educators today borrow from both lists in recognition that the musical processes are what are constant, not musical repertoires. Satisfactory musical performance counts more than some single, sanctioned method of reaching this goal. Facts about music are less important than one's capacity to find the facts one needs to understand some musical event or another. Music educators use both sides of the list because this knowledge and these skills and values represent valid, widely used approaches to musical success, approaches used in both populist and elitist traditions. In using approaches from a variety of traditions, music educators attempt to stand astride the musical culture—to bring all of it into the school.

Music educators have paid a heavy price for this new stance. They feel that there has been a loss of support from both segments of the society, the elites as well as the general populace. The political dilemma of the modern music educator is to be enough of an elitist to have the social elites' support, and to be enough of a populist to draw students to their elective classes, to fill their performing groups' rosters, and to entertain their audiences.

MUSIC IN BARBERSHOPPING AND EDUCATION

Taken as a form of human musical behavior, barbershop music can trace its roots to the prehistory of Western civilization. The earthy moralism of the Homeric ballads became coupled with the notion, recognized by both Plato and Aristotle, that the ballads' musical settings themselves had moral consequences. This provided vernacular musicians of the last two or three millennia with their ground rules: either celebrate life or moralize about living it, but stay solidly within the composition's moral and musical traditions. In current times, the sentimental songs of the 19th century Euro-American parlor—moral epithets and parables clothed in simple but interesting harmonies and manageable tunes—flowed naturally into what is now known as barbershop. The arrangement of voice parts in the ensemble (tenor, lead, baritone, bass) has been common practice for centuries in America and is found in other vernacular musics, most notably traditional country and western commercial music. Barbershop music today, as a set of songs and musical composition and performance habits, traces its roots to the Victorian parlor and the recreational improvisations of gentlemen at leisure, in fraternal organizations and social clubs.

What barbershoppers are really preserving, perhaps without knowing it, is even more valuable than their songs. It is not reflected in artifacts of words and music. It is reflected, rather in the human use to which they are put. Barbershopping, especially quartet singing, is arguably the last extant example in American culture of the ancient tradition of secular vocal parlor musics. Parlor music is personal music of manageable proportions, bestowing its benefits socially through the music in the performer by self-producing social closeness with a few others. Unfortunately, no important relic of this tradition remains in living American musical culture, except perhaps for today's barbershoppers' practices, an observation explored in some detail by Peter Etzkorn elsewhere in this volume. The "hootenannies" of the 1950s and 1960s failed to self-generate a genre, either musical or social, although it is common for professional vocal entertainers such as Harry Belafonte or "The Nylons" to get an audience singing. Campfire songs and shape-note singing, and barbershopping, at least, retain much of vernacular parlor singing's *gemütlichkeit* character; but only barbershop quartet singing preserves for common folk the possibility that these benefits can be managed in taxicabs, basement recreation rooms, and hotel lobbies. (See Max Brandt's chapter in this book for details.) There are some current instrumental "parlor" musics, mainly realized in pick-up string quartets, on front porches in the rural South, and in the teenage rock band's family garage. Some older secular vocal parlor musics such as madrigal singing are being preserved, museum-like, for display to the curious and to the aficionado.

Here is what surprises this music educator: Because barbershopping comes from parlor entertainment roots, and because barbershoppers derive most of their benefits from the comradeship that parlor singing has always generated, it is surprising that barbershoppers seem so willing to risk losing this benefit by seeking large public venues as a means of keeping their tradition alive. If the tradition is parlor singing, then its benefits cannot be found in large auditoriums. Nor can it be realized by sitting in an audience and listening. Either barbershoppers' values are truly shifting or the large-scale means of realizing them are beginning to create necessities out of virtues that have nothing to do with the traditions that guaranteed barbershopping's benefits. Comradeship develops in theatre companies, too; but this is qualitatively different from that which develops in parlor music. Barbershoppers who pursue public performance success feel theatrical social benefits rather than those of the parlor. One is not necessarily better than the other, but they produce different behaviors and derive their benefits from different sources.

Today, barbershop music's social benefits are derived from two powerful but competing sources: one source demands attention to an entertainer's craft (presentation quality, comedy routines, production values, etc.), and a second source demands attention to the musical artifacts associated with barbershop music of years gone by. Barbershop music, well presented, is entertaining, and one knows a barbershop song when one hears it. It is also entertaining (for a while) to watch an artist painting a picture on a city street. Public television's list of top programs includes those that show expert carpenters, cooks, craftsmen, and fishermen working at their trades. Interest in these is an accident of time and taste, both of which march on. Entertainment and repertoire are not the core of the barbershop (or craft, or culinary) tradition. To preserve the core, barbershoppers must accept as fortuitously accidental the fact that some people find their activity entertaining. This must be reduced to secondary importance if vocal parlor music benefits are to be preserved by barbershoppers. There is also danger in holding to some sort of assumed musical purity of the barbershopper's repertoire. Adherents to this conservative view must also realize that the sociopersonal benefits that lie at the core of barbershopping can be realized with other music than what is rigidified by the rules of international quartet competitions.

Neither a specific set of musical artifacts nor the entertainment crafts truly matter in the preservation of the barbershopping tradition. It is personal, vernacular, manageable but imaginative music-making that matters. It is on this value that American music educators and barbershoppers stand united.

THE TAG

The quest for insightful, even profound, music occupies musical performers of all traditions, in and out of educational institutions. Most of what is composed in a given month, of course, fails to achieve memorability. The standard repertoire in any genre has survived a merciless gauntlet of critics. In this critical sense, all musicians and music consumers are elitist. In matters of musical taste, minimally experienced performers and listeners know what they like and can stratify what they know. Elitism and musical taste are not merely parallel issues here; they are connected. Choosing one musical work over another gives public expression to taste and taste provides evidence of musical status. Status and the perceived need for it, coupled with choices of musical works and performance activity, provide the fuel for stratifying groups of musicians. The status of music educators and barbershoppers as segments of the worldwide community of musicians is of concern to both groups.

The relationship among groups of musicians, then, is a status relationship, a relationship rooted in culture and played out in society. It is displayed in choices of music and, to a more lasting degree, in preferred, patterned, preserved choices of educational and performance activity. All of this happens to real people, in "leisure frameworks" (see Phillip Bosserman's chapter in this volume) that weave music making intimately in the fabric with the other parts of their lives.

If barbershoppers succeed in gaining entree to the music education establishment, barbershoppers risk weakening the connection with populist musical and social values that has supported the progress of the movement to date. Institutionalized barbershopping (The SPEBSQSA, Sweet Adelines International, etc.) has a vital interest in preserving barbershopping's core values and has intricate, well-developed mechanisms for doing so. Music educators have much to learn from the barbershop movement about these mechanisms. They also have a responsibility to learn what they can about barbershop singing as a manageable form of personal music making—about its "woodshedding" practices, its benefits and costs, its musical treasures, its ways of drawing people of good will into its unified body. Much of this is available in SPEBSQSA's chapter craft and musical leadership materials and educational processes—Chapter Officers' Training Schools (COTS), Harmony College, judges' training courses, etc. Sweet Adelines International has well-developed regional structures for coaching struggling chapters and for training the undeveloped adult female voice. Both the Society and Harmony, Inc. have successful and practical methods of helping their members to learn singing techniques indigenous to the style. Music educators teach such content, also, but to children and youth.

Barbershop organizations have leadership help that many music educators need. The status relationship of the two groups, however, dictates that neither one sees the other as having something to offer that the other group needs. Currently, SPEBSQSA rents booths at music educators' conventions, offers a Young Men in Harmony newsletter, sells school-level music and audio tapes, organizes high school barbershop festivals, and visits schools. In 1971 the Music Educators National Conference (MENC) approved a barbershop quartet category in school music contests. This was a rather empty gesture and not too much should be expected as a result of it. Most music contests and festivals are run by state organizations independently of the MENC, even though all but Texas are units of MENC. Music educators can offer trained musical assistance when barbershoppers need technical help, they can provide supervision and access to school performance spaces, and they teach a pool of potential future barbershop participants.

Will there be an ongoing connection between barbershoppers and music educators? Perhaps. But, it is likely to continue for the present as a commercial one—music and tapes from barbershoppers, inexpensive performance spaces from the music educators. As the number of these interactions multiply, however, doorways to other interactions of more substance will be opened. Should barbershoppers adopt institutionalized music education's values and practices? No. Doing so would imperil barbershopping's strong identification with vernacular music-making. Should barbershoppers staunchly defend the "old songs" against creeping progressivism of newer styles of vocal ensemble singing? No. This is not what is important about barbershopping.

Culturally, music education and barbershopping occupy different spaces—music education attempts to embrace all important American musical traditions in some way: barbershopping is one of those traditions. The traditions of both groups include ways of preserving monuments of musical traditions; and these ways of preserving are part of the monuments. To the degree that both barbershopping and music education preserve their characteristics, to that degree they are different enterprises and depend for their support on their separate claims to uniqueness.

References

Blair, John G. (1988). *Modular America: Cross-cultural Perspectives on the Emergence of an American Way.* Westport, CT: Greenwood.

Gates, J. Terry. (1990a). *Ferme la porte?:* On Michael L. Mark's "A New Look at Historical Periods in American Music Education." *Bulletin of the Council for Research in Music Education, 103,* 29–34.

Gates, J. Terry. (1990b). Music education's Professional Beginnings in America: Early Eighteenth-Century New England Singing-School Teacher Qualifications and Program Goals. *The Quarterly, I* (1 & 2), 43–48.

Haack, Paul. (1987). The Question of Elitism: Some Movement to the Left? *Bulletin of the Council for Research in Music Education, 93,* 19–22.

Kaplan, Max. (1990). *The Arts: A Social Perspective.* Rutherford, NJ: Fairleigh Dickinson University.

Levine, Walter. (1988). *Highbrow/Lowbrow: The Emergence of Cultural Hierarchy in America.* Cambridge, MA: Harvard University Pres.

Salmen, Walter, ed. (1983). *The Social Status of the Professional Musician from the Middle Ages to the 19th Century.* New York: Pendragon Press.

Small, Christopher. (1987). *Music of the Common Tongue.* London: John Calder; New York: Riverrun Press.

Temperley, Nicholas. (1981). The Old Way of Singing: Its Origins and Development. *American Musicological Society Journal, 34* (3), 511–44.

Warner, W. Lloyd. (1949). *Social Class in America—a Manual of Procedure for the Measurement of Social Status.* Chicago: Science Research Associates.

Barbershoppers as Vestige of the Past and Promise for the Future: On Live Music Making in America

K. PETER ETZKORN

Barbershoppers represent a special category of music aficionados; they are among the minority of North Americans who favor live music. In the company of similarly dedicated individuals, they devote hours of leisure time honing vocal skills, faithfully practicing and perfecting their live musical performance. They learn the specific musical criteria of this type of choral music and learn how to apply them in refining their specialized harmonic sound production. Typically their vocal music making is *a capella*, unfettered by artificial pitch constraints of other musical instruments than their own voices. In performance they control their own pitches by listening to the pitches simultaneously sounded by their fellow music makers. In some sense theirs is a preindustrial type of musical culture that coexists with the many varieties of musical sounds in our world. In another sense, this survival of real music whose musical soundscape is composed largely of sounds fabricated through loudspeakers, contains certain socio-musical dimensions which on analysis might help us discern what are the more lasting elements of an active musical culture.

The Media World of Music

Anyone making a survey of musical life in the United States will be challenged by the tremendous quantity of musical sounds that will be encountered. Most of these, however, will not come from a live musical source, of an individual or a group of musicians singing or playing instruments. Most musical sounds, instead, will come from loudspeakers. Indeed, some of these occur at such a level of volume that their presence may cause physical damage to hearing organs not unlike other noises characteristic of our technological age. To safeguard individuals from such harm, protective measures have been promoted by the United States government. America is noisier than ever today. But not everyone objects to the propagation of noise. Dr. Ernest A. Peterson of the University of Miami School of Medicine, a leading authority on the physiological effects of noise, stated: "We know that the level of sound produced by 'boom box' radios and tape players elevates blood levels of norepinephrine—adrenaline. There's evidence that some people enjoy the highs they get from adrenaline."[1]

In today's world musical sounds are everywhere and most of them radiate from loudspeakers. Music is heard by anxious fathers in the waiting room of hospitals when mothers give birth to their infants; it is heard in the hallways of funeral parlors when the bereaved gather to honor the dead. Department stores, dentists' offices, airplanes prior to take off and after landing, hotel lobbies and dining rooms count among the many sites which customarily are enveloped in music as if it were part of the furnishings or built into its surrounding as wallpaper. If music were to be absent, it would strike many as odd; silence would be intolerable. Thus we are attuned to its ever presence.

When we attempt to describe the typical characteristics of these situations in the 1990s in which music forms an integral part of the ecology, we will point to their common elements of electronically amplified sounds that spring from loudspeakers or are transmitted through earphones. Typically their source is the playback of a prior recording session of live music. Less frequently loudspeakers are also used to amplify the music making of live musicians, as when rock musicians connect their instruments with amplifiers and other electronic hardware to modify their volume and tonal characteristics and to diffuse the sound more widely; thus they make themselves heard through loudspeakers.

Another way of describing the typical musical situation is by recognizing that the majority of musical sounds in today's world are mediated through loudspeakers. As a consequence, most people experience music most of the time through the playback of previously recorded sounds via radio or television receivers, record players, tape recorders (either audio or video), or compact disc players. In this manner, musical experiences for most people are receptive; they hinge on the state of media technology, and encompass only limited personal and musical activity. This contrasts with settings in which individuals themselves make music solo or in concert with others, combining musical activity simultaneously with reception.

In quantitative terms the majority of all musical sounds in our environment are electronically amplified and diffused through loudspeakers. Earphones, the smaller cousins of loudspeakers, bring sounds to individual listeners. We need to remember that the original sources recorded for musical reproduction are one-time live musical events. They are preserved for repeated soundings, encrypted on cassett audio or video tapes, compact or long-playing discs, and electronically amplified and played back through audio or video broadcasts, individual tape, or disc players. Typically, such recording media stretch the outreach of an original "performance" to a multiple of size of audience that might have attended the occasion of the recording session. This is easly recognized when one considers that the recordings of live crowd events, even as large as Woodstock, reach far larger numbers of future record buyers and repeat listeners than could have heard the musicians perform live. Even more so studio recordings, the staple of the industry, clearly reach larger numbers of record listeners than could be accommodated as the audience within a recording studio.

The industrialization of musical life has been analyzed by Kurt Blaukopf and his associates and characterized by *mediamorphosis* (Blaukopf, 1989:4),[2] Audience responses to media music typically are similar to the reception of other mass-produced goods, in which the public receives the goods ready-made to be used off the shelves, without further or at most very limited creative or re-creative efforts. Those exposed to media music typically hear sounds that come from loudpseakers (or earphones) and, equally typically, have little awareness or interest in understanding the technological processes by which these sounds were codified and then reproduced. Typically there is some commercial connection between the initial recording, mechanical and electronic packaging, and eventual distribution of the recorded product, as when an initial performance is packaged as a cassette tape, promoted by a recording company in conjunction with video productions, sold in music stores and then available for playback at will by the purchaser.

Whether it is classified as "classic," "popular," "jazz," or even "religious,"[3] in quantitative terms most music is physically diffused, sounded and received via recordings through loudspeakers. The actual making of music by barbershops clearly takes on an unusual form of what is typically sounded and experienced as music by the vast publics in postindustrial life.

Communal Dimensions of Barbershop Music

Barbershop music is different from the vast majority of contemporary musical presentations in at least two respects. First, it is *live music* and as such has unique musical dimensions whenever it is sounded. No single live musical phrase when sounded again can be said to be as exact a copy of its previous rendition than one can say about the multiple playback of recorded sound track when each playback is musically indistinguishable from its prior rendition. Consider, for example, that singers vary their intonation, treatment of note values, enunciation and stress on vowels and consonants, blending and phrasing, tonal attack, changes in tempo and volume, and even the timbre of their sound formation. Each time a piece or phrase is repeated there will be some variation in one or the other of these dimensions. Second, as live vocal music, it also has characteristic social dimensions which are absent from mechanically reproduced mediated music. *Mediated music* does not require the participation of other musicians once it has been recorded. Its playback may even be enjoyed by an individual via quadrophonic earphones in splendid isolation from any other individual, with the recorded sounds reverberating in private in the cranial cavities.

Barbershop music making, by definition, cannot take place in splendid isolation: it requires the participation of a group of fellow singers. They are involved in musical give and take, whether in rehearsal or in performance, and their individual focus on their joint musical accomplishments also makes them subjugate their outside, non-musical, persona to their common musical goal. Whether physician, lawyer or laborer, their roles, functions and accomplishments in the barbershop setting are defined by their shared musical aesthetic. Here they are singing the lead, or harmonize above the melody as tenor, with the bass providing the lowest harmonizing line and the baritone completing the harmonic structure either below or above the melody.

As a community of musicians they share in the dicta of a musical aesthetic which is centrally oriented towards support of barbershop harmony. Publications of the Society for the Preservation and Encouragement of Barber Shop Quartet Singing in America, provide various descriptions of the style:

> Barbershop music features major and minor chords and barbershop (dominant type) seventh chords, resolving primarily on the circle of fifths. Sixths, ninth, and major seventh chords are avoided except where demanded by the melody, while chords containing the minor second interval are not used. The basic harmonization may be embellished with additional chord progressions to provide harmonic interest and rhythmic momentum, to carry over between phrases, or to introduce or close the song effectively (SPEBSQSA, 1987:20).

In order to perfect this barbershop sound, learning the intervals for the harmonic parts of a song in rehearsal with the aid of tempered instruments is frowned upon. The chord relationships which are obtained by blending the vocal parts are often quite at variance with those that would be derived from fixed pitch instruments which makes for the easy recognition of the barbershop style harmonies. The reason, of course, is that fixed pitch instruments employ the equal tempered scale but that the actual notes sung will vary as much as six to ten cycles per second depending on the harmony part's interval relationship to the melodic part (Huff, n.d.:4).

Other aesthetic choices that are shared within the musical community of barbershop singers deal with the production of: expanded sound, which adds to the quality of intonation, through such factors as uniformity of word sounds in good quality, proper volume relationships between voice parts, precision of execution, and synchronization of word sounds; interpretation, or the emotional impact created by the singers with artistic use of good vocal technique; and stage presence, or the overall rapport the singers develop with their audience, their visual interpretation of the mood/message within the song, and the appropriate and effective use of costuming. These criteria form a fundamental set of shared understandings in the barbershop community. They are refined into explicit standards for judging the performances during quartet competitions.

By practicing to make their musical performances conform to these aesthetic criteria, barbershoppers at once share in an elemental source of social and musical compact. As an active musical community, therefore, they can easily be distinguished from the many publics of mediated music both by their shared involvement in live music making and the consistent adherence to an explicit (aesthetic) normative structure that binds them together.

We will return to a further exploration of the special roles of barbershop music for the future of live music, after we explore some of the problems which we ascribe to the domineering reliance on loudspeaker and media music in our contemporary society.

Sociological Thoughts on Media Music

Not all barbershop music is sounded in live performances. Audio and video recordings of prize winning quartets are available for mediated playback as are those of choruses and of special occasions such as joint performances with the Mormon Tabernacle Choir. The barbershop numbers of "The Iowa Four" in *The Music Man* original cast recording reached wide audiences as did appearances by various quartets on network television variety shows. There is a sizable audience for barbershop music as can be gleaned from a recent study for the National Endowment for the Arts. An estimated one million adult Americans were expected to respond that they liked barbershop music best (Horowitz, 1986:58). This is about the same number who prefer Opera. Barbershop music, hence, joins the great variety of mediated music from rock 'n roll, pop, gospel, to symphony broadcasts that dominates our musical soundscape, and in its mediated form it demands to be examined for various sociological consequences. Precisely through such analyses will an understanding of the significance of the social nature of barbershop music be gained for its potential contribution to our musical future.

It is quite true that with the arrival of digitized recording and compact disc playback technology, the reproductive fidelity of recorded sound becomes hard to distinguish for the untutored ear from the sound of live performances. Many commentators regard this as testimony to technological progress. Naturally, many of these are promoters for the recording industry and entertainment conglomerates which have a financial stake in the commercialization of recordings. This motivation cannnot be imputed to the aesthetician John Mowitt who in his searching paper "Music in the Era of Electronic Reproducibility" extends Walter Benjamin's classic analysis of art in the era of technological reproducibility to music (Benjamin, 1936). He goes as far as to suggest that "the compact disc player promises not only to supersede the claims of reproductive fidelity made by Memorex, but to integrate, at the level of a technological continuum, the modes of production, reproduction and reception . . . At that point the contrast between what is 'live' and what is Memorex will be irrelevant" (Mowitt, 1987:193). His reference to Memorex speaks to a television advertisement for blank recording tape in which listeners ostensibly cannot distinguish whether the sound they hear comes from a live performance or its playback on Memorex tape. Sociological commentators, however, are not as sanguine that perfection in recording techniques implies the attainment of unquestioned artistic benefits. They consider a "musical situation" to implicate creators, performers, and listeners. They also note that advances in high fidelity have wrought social changes whose consequences do not necessarily bode well either for the presence or the future of live music. For a moment, without exploring the full panoply of sociological rationale, consider the narrow question of what would constitute an appropriate acknowledgment for composers and performers of recorded works that become a bestseller?

If each playback were treated identically to a repeat live performance, their recognition certainly would include critical reactions and applause of their audiences, not to speak of each audience member possibly contributing financially to each live musical event through the purchase of a ticket. In a live performance, artists and audience would be united in time and space. But this is not so for hi-fi playback when the original performers are without any interactive relationship with the individual members—their size, locations, and make up of their audiences. As Besseler remarked during his introductory lecture about music in the new era at Freiburg University in 1925: "Through radio, the public is expanded into an unlimited, totally atomized mass. The gramophone, in addition, annuls any common temporal connection."[4] Sociologists would agree with Besseler's contention. Moreover, they would expect that many essential dimensions of the social situation of live music making between musicians and their audiences would not be encrypted on the Memorex tape, and hence that the social aesthetic dimensions of live music making and of high fidelity playback of mediated music are drastically different (Etzkorn, 1989: 125–35). Barbershoppers performing or listening to their concerts, of course, also know this and spend many hours in rehearsal to perfect their musical and social stage presentation with their audience in mind.

While it is consistent with the marketing perspective of promoters of the music industry, it is somewhat surprising that neither musicologists, performing musicians, music educators or aestheticians differentiate a great deal between live and loudspeaker mediated music. It is truly surprising that promoters and program annotators even for stellar performance events such as the appearance of international soloists with major United States symphony orchestras, will enlist the vocabulary of media representatives by emphasizing rave notices about the manufacturer, number and prizes awarded for recordings made by the artist, as if the forthcoming live performance had anything in common with the artificially spliced together recording media industrially packaged for mass marketing.

Barbershop singers, as well as other performing musicians and their conductors, instead, know that the acoustic qualities of different performance sites introduce sufficient challenges that they need to adapt their music making to such changing conditions as variations in reverberation times, or hall acoustics that selectively resonate to certain pitches, to mention some of the more obvious differences. What one might like to learn from advance publicity about unfamiliar performers, then, would be how well they coped with performing in different halls, with different conductors, and how audiences in other communities received their playing. Such reports would tell the reader something about the musical competencies of the travelling artists under changing performance conditions. That so-and-so received a Grammy Award, of course, also speaks to something about the recorded performance. But in the case of recorded productions it is not immediately clear whether it speaks more to the public relations and marketing efforts of the business managers of the record company, to judgments about the performers' artistic abilities to function within the peculiar setting of a recording session, the expertise of the musical engineering staff in creating balances among the parts recorded on different sound tracks, the placement of microphones, or the editing of various recording "takes" into the final recorded version for commercial release. It is not clear at all why readers are given this information or how they are to react and convert it meaningfully into musical expectancies about future live performances. What is clear, however, is that commercial criteria about mediated music for loudspeakers are uncritically appropriated by these writers over aesthetic judgments more pertinent to live performances. Barbershop musicians in making music are conscious of such distinctions. They and their coaches are reminded that adaptation to changing environments and variation in musical execution matter for their quartets and choruses, and that "good stage presence enhances the interpretative sounds so as to add to the meanings of words more effectively" (Huff, n.d.:7).

For the barbershop community, while inundated like everybody else by media fabricated loudspeaker sounds, there is little argument about the basic observation that there are important differences between the social situation of loudspeaker and performed, live music. For them, the making of live music offers both musical and social challenges. In meeting these challenges head on, they represent a minority position in the community. They are ahead of either musicologists, music educators, sociologists, or performing musicians who in their writings scarcely differentiate between live and loudspeaker mediated music. Except for discourse that focuses on music specifically conceived for loudspeaker dissemination, such as computer and electronic music, most of these writers treat all music indiscriminately of its source in live or mediated performance.

We may speculate on reasons for this relative inattention to what barbershoppers know to be essential dimensions of live music. One reason may well be that the preoccupation among academic musicologists has not been with performance but with the analysis of notated scores and archival documents about music. Whether a piece is sounded by instruments or by loudspeakers adds little insight to the musicological analysis of the notated score of a composition, and whether a score discovered in an archive has ever been realized in performance and under what specific sounding conditions, is frequently disregarded by traditional musicology (Etzkorn, 1988:45).

And in the field of music education, loudspeaker reproduction has become a convenient substitute for live music. It makes it possible for teachers to reduce their own labors (or, perhaps, to disguise their own musical inadequacies) by not preparing live musical illustrations. By playing recordings through loudspeakers, they would conveniently bring a wealth of loudspeaker simulations of musical sitautions right into the conventional classroom environment to enrich their instruction; they may even require "listening assignments" from a sound archive for their students (Etzkorn, 1990). And, as many publicists for live musical events employ references to the sales success of recorded music to distend their case, the writers on music education are similar to musicologists in not questioning seriously whether there are pedagogical limitations of dependency on these media. Not unlike barbershoppers, Wes Blomster, the philosopher, remarks about loudspeaker music's power to communicate with an audience: "Insofar as the experience of [loudspeaker] music today involves communication at all, it is a one way process, involving passive acceptance on the part of the listener" (Blomster, 1977:77).

We see that neither sociologists nor the majority of the musical community have entertained much serious inquiry into either the differences between live and mediated music or the consequences of the predominance of mediated music for the future of the community of musical performers. While the specter of technological unemployment through the use of media music instead of live performance might cause musicians to search for ways to promote live over media music, and thereby to portray media music as radically different from live music, most of what there is in the form of organized reaction accepts media music as a given and valid form of musical expression. Rather than demanding that live performances of music replace loudspeaker music and offer them further employment, recent actions by organized musicians have almost exclusively been directed towards securing increased economic benefits from one time recording sessions, such as through concessions for mechanical rights through royalty payments for the repeated playback of recordings. To the extent that they were successful in such negotiations, loudspeaker music becomes a useful and immediate extension of their own art so that they do not become concerned with its social impact and the potentially hazardous repercussions for the future of the wider community of musicians. While this high degree of individualism may be puzzling, many years ago Hanns Eisler offered a possible explanation for why musical performers acquiescently comply with changing technological circumstances of musical life. He referred to the musicians' "traditional role of 'rendering service'—in Germany, orchestra players speak of *Abenddienst*" with a consequent mania to please and a zealous pandering to what the audience wants (Eisler, 1947:48).

As far as the sociological literature is concerned, its coverage until recently appears not to have differed from the topics treated in musicology. Most analyses were equally conventional by their focus on explaining the social role of composers, and in analyzing the function of works of music and of their authenticity, or the influence of social conditions on musical details (Rummenhöller, 1978:50). The fact that the "typical" musical situation in the United States, the most usual, involving the most people in music, is receptive and mediated through loudspeakers has attracted little attention. Of course, this is not to say that there is not a sociological literature which describes the economic power of the media and analyzes how industrial and commercial interests affect the marketing and distribution of loudspeaker music via the various broadcast media, or record and video producers. But this literature only marginally sheds light on such key questions about the sociological nature of the social situation of the recording session and its participants, as their recruitment, selection, education, familial support, aesthetic and musical socialization, performance skills, status. Clearly, without musicians having acquired the musical competencies for performing in recording sessions, there would not be any way for the music business to record and market anything.

Loudspeaker Music versus Barbershop Music

Loudspeakers allow for the diffusion of sounds that were electronically manipulated and because a "sonic commodity which embeds itself in physical matter in a manner not possible in performed music" (Fergson, 1983:22). Mediated music, once it is recorded, can be played back at will, out of sequence, and it does not allow for any musically creative interpretative variation in playback other than perhaps an electronic manipulation of the originally recorded sound track. While it results from performance, it "exists as something other than performance" (Ferguson, 1983:24). In the playback of recorded music, there is no place for musical performers who, as Collingswood saw it in live performances, function as coauthors of the composer, when through their individual execution they develop the aesthetic implications of a musical composition (Collingswood, 1958:328).

The singers in a barbershop quartet or chorus do not reply on sounds recorded for secondary consumption; they themselves make the music come alive through direct personal participation in a group setting. Individually and collectively, they are involved in the selection of their fellow quartet members as well as of the musical repertoire to be studied and performed. They exercise control over the degree of musical difficulty of musical arrangements for the individual pieces and the overall program and they pay attention that the lyrics are regarded to be "in good taste." As individual singers they are given the opportunity to exercise leadership in a group setting where their musical ability will be recognized and reinforced by their fellow singers. They show off their individual talents in their pursuit of the common musical goal of barbershop harmony which requires that every performer fuse his voice to blend in with the voices of every other quartet member to harmonize the lead's melody in "barbershop chord" structure. As a consequence of such close musical articulation, it is more likely than not that every repeat performance of one and the same piece is different in some musical degree from previous ones.

From the musical criteria of paying close attention to each other, shared understandings from building a social community of barbershoppers across conventional boundaries of social status, differentiation and taste groupings have developed. The governing criteria for acceptance in this community are explicitly musical and any variation in status is expressed in similar terms. Supportive evidence is easily found in barbershop idioms and jokes. Barbershop music, indeed, means the making of live music in which performers, using the prior creative output of composers and arrangers, through social interaction, make musical scores come alive for themselves and for their audiences. This is how music has been made throughout history, until the development and continuous improvement of sound recording apparatus in this century has given rise to the widely held illusion that recorded and live musics are one and the same.

Barbershop Music is Real, Not an Illusion

When adapting Walter Benjamin's quest for the locus of authenticity in visual art to music, Wes Blomster asked "But in music, does authenticity lie in the composition itself, or is it rather present in the realization of the score in performance" (Blomster, 1977:66)? For Collingswood, this question would have been answered through his observation that "what is on paper is not music, it is only musical notation" (Collingswood, 1958:135). By analogy we would reason that what is encrypted on a musical recording is similar to musical notation. Instead of written, it is a collection of electronic instructions for the reproduction of fixed acoustic relationships and their possible amplification through loudspeakers. When a recording is played back it will not be further modified or coauthored by performers. The playback apparatus only obeys the signals that were preserved on it and reproduce, with more or less fidelity, the sounds of a one-time musical event. Listeners may imagine that they partake in this original performance, but unlike their presence at a live performance, there is no way in which they may interact with the performing musicians, neither through gestures of pleasant approval nor expressions of critical disgust.

At barbershop performances, not only is the interaction between performers and audience a constant reminder of its being *live* music, but so is the vocal and gestural give and take among the singers. Singers play to the audience and to each other, and the audience responds with applause, laughter, gestures, and, perhaps, occasional signs of critical disapproval. For those present, barbershop music is real, full of excitement and expressive energy, not an illusion.

Prospects

The recent history of popular music in America has largely been a history of changes in the labelling and marketing of recorded sound packages. Musical groups come and go. Bands and vocalists are selected and promoted by record manufacturers consistent with their objective to sell recordings and to create more demand for more sales of recorded products. These can be multiplied ad infinitum. Mediamorphosis through radio and recordings also has affected such other performing fields as opera, chamber and symphonic music. And their records are marketed by the same entertainment conglomerates and sold through the same distribution channels. The economic fusion of record, video, radio, cinema, and print media dealing with music makes it necessary to acknowledge the common dominance of recorded sounds and loudspeaker music in our culture. All musical styles today are represented on records.

Along with church choirs, amateur chamber music groups, jazz ensembles, community bands and professional orchestras, barbershop singers are among the few who keep on creating live music in America. And along with these, barbershoppers perform an historic mission, the preservation of a capella vocal group music, with a style free of the artificial constraints of the tempered scale. Self-consciously they practice their musical art again and again, and are not deceived through illusions of loudspeaker playback as taking the place of music.

When considering the future of barbershop music, it is illuminating to ask how this musical form has persisted so far. What characteristics can be identified that kept this form of live music and its aesthetic alive during a time when most other music has become mediated?

Among the outstanding features of the staying power of barbershop music in the age of loudspeaker music, no doubt, must be counted its emphasis on collective music making that fuses identifiable individual contributions into a vehicle for communal participation and recognition. Then there is the sharing of explicit technical criteria of voice, pitch, harmonic production, and of the somewhat less precise aesthetic criteria about the creation of "proper" barbershop music as these are reinforced through judges at competitions, who foster a "musical reward system" for improved performances. To work towards and attain these communal values requires personal dedication to the joint goals of the quartets and choruses. This dedication may even become a focal point in the organization of the everyday lives of individual barbershop singers (see chapter by Robert A. Stebbins in this collection). Clearly, barbershop music making requires personal effort, dedication, and the refinement through practice of a combination of social and musically creative and receptive skills.

The world of live barbershop music may well be surviving in the age of mediamorphosis because its aficionados are actively pursuing both creative and receptive efforts. The organization of their musical activities offers social-psychological supports for being simultaneously musically creative and receptive. Cognitive psychology tells us that clearly not everyone excels at functioning in both of these psychological dimensions, and clearly not everyone could be the creative giant of a Mozart. But the ways in which barbershop activities are organized, from the recruitment of new members and the coaching of quartets, through the musical workshops at Harmony College specifically designed for improving the musicianship of barbershop singers—provide ongoing communal supports for the musical and personal self-development of creative and receptive skills. Individual barbershoppers find themselves challenged to meet the musical expectations of their fellow members within an institutional framework that assists their personal growth towards this communal goal of making good barbershop music.

It would appear that whereas media music thrives from maximizing impersonal sales of recorded musical commodities in the depersonalized world of the lonely crowd, barbershop music thrives because it is performed and enjoyed in communal settings. Moreover, where novelty and turnover of styles along with improvements of media technology are among the trademarks of media music, barbershop musicians work at refining its traditional style and at adapting newer musical material to become consistent with its form. And where discussions of media music tend to de-emphasize concern with live music—as when a record company declines to record a band because it is composed of black and white musicians and, therefore, is assumed not to be able to appeal to either the black or white rock 'n roll audience—the set of instructions for judging barbershop competitions explicitly deals with musical qualifications rather than the skin color of the singers. Finally, where media music severely limits the range of musical expression by relying so exclusively on the technological potential of the loudspeaker as instrument for the production of sound, barbershop music is built on the most versatile of instruments for the expression of musical emotion: the human voice.

Conclusions

Barbershop singing in today's world represents a special form of musical activity. There are other musical organizations that also practice live choral singing and attract a following of amateur and professional musicians. Most of these, like the barbershoppers, count on individual musicians to contribute their art to the cause of music, and most participants derive personal satisfactions from thus giving of their leisure time. Here we will only refer to another organized form of vocal music which attracts publics for singing aloud and which appears to be commercially rewarding. *Singalong* has recently become financially successful and remained so over an extended period. Singalong takes place in one huge room, with video monitors hanging overhead, and a sound system providing loudspeaker accompaniment for the singing. "Lyric sheets" are unscrolled on Singalong's monitors while emcees encourage patrons to get up on stage and entertain their fellow audience members. There is an admission charge and additional revenue derives from the sale of food and beverages. Singalong turned into such success on Manhattan's West 19th Street that an Atlanta branch has already been opened and others are being planned to be opened. "If you get five guys or five girls up there, it's fun and it's safe. You get the thrill of being on stage, but you feel like your friends can help carry you" (Spayde, 1990:50). In a different vein, open rehearsals of standard choral pieces conducted by noted choral conductors are advertised for an admission charge of $10 to appeal to "Bring the entire choir! . . . Bring 10 people, get one free admission."[5]

It appears that active singing, when attractively packaged, can be promoted to become commercially successful. While the pool of potential participants from which to draw on may be much smaller, the fact that live vocal music competes with loudspeaker music in the commercial arena suggests that it is a persistent aspect of contemporary musical culture. Moreover, since through its musical form it fosters sociability even among otherwise isolated individuals, those musical organizations which, like the barbershoppers, explicitly combine specific musical with social organizational requirements are likely to experience mutual reinforcement between musical and social norms. Following this line of sociological reasoning, the barbershop community is well positioned to continue to attract and hold the commitment of singers and live music aficionados who will practice and enjoy their art while the world around them is inundated by loudspeaker sounds which are manipulated by industrial marketeers and even public relations representatives of symphonic and concert organizations. This writer has the hope that once commercial interests discover that there is a stable audience for live music that is willing to put resources into it, they may recognize not only that the future of the recording industry is tied up with maintaining a reservoir of performing musicians but that their economic self-interest may even be served by self-consciously promoting musical and social criteria of live music groups.

Barbershoppers and their musical style are likely to have a more stable future than any of the many musical groups that at one or the other moment in recent history are riding high on the promotional waves of the fickle recording industry. To build a growing market for their products, the recording industry might even look to barbershop music as a model of how to survive and prosper.

Notes

1. "Research on Noise Disappears In the Din," *The New York Times*, March 6, 1990, B 5, C.1.
2. Anthropologists introduced the distinction between "art by destination" (involving direct appreciation by an audience) and "art by metamorphosis" which involves delayed appreciation due to changing standards or preferences of the audience. Music which is composed to be "performed" and then appreciated through a recording would be an illustration of art by metamorphosis (Maquet, 1971).
3. The use of recorded music at religious ceremonies is not restricted to, while perhaps most frequently found in, funeral parlors.
4. As quoted in Blaukopf, (1989:4), [author's translation].
5. Advertisement in the St. Louis Post Dispatch: "Sing with Roger Wagner.

Choir singers and directors Sing the Fauré Requiem in a giant rehearsal conducted by Roger Wagner, Admission is $10 per person."

References

Benjamin, Walter. 1936. "Das Kunstwerk im Zeitalter seiner technischen Reproduzierbarkeit." *Zeitschrift für Sozialforschung.*

Blaukopf, Kurt. 1989. *Beethovens Erben in der Mediamorphose: Kultur- und Medienpolitik für die elektronische Ära.* Musik und Gesellschaft. Heiden: Verlag Arthur Niggli. xxi + 175p.

Blomster, Wes V. 1977. "Electronic music." *Telos,* 32 (Summer): 65–78.

Collingswood, R. G. 1958. *The Principles of Art.* A Galaxy Book GB11. New York: Oxford University Press. xxi + 347p.

Eisler, Hanns. 1947. *Composing for the films.* New York: Oxford University Press. xi + 165p.

Etzkorn, K. Peter. 1990. "Contemporary Mediated Music: Challenge to Music Education." *International Journal of Music Education,* 16:3–12.

Etzkorn, K. Peter. 1989. "On Loudspeakers and the Sociology of Music." Chapter in Walter Nutz. *Kunst, Kommunikation, Kultur: Festschrift zum 80. Geburtstag von Alphons Silbermann.* pp. 125–35. Bern: Verlag Peter Lang.

Etzkorn, K. Peter. 1988. "Publications and their Influence on the Development of Ethnomusicology." *Yearbook for Traditional Music,* 20:43–50.

Ferguson, Linda. 1983. "Tape Composition: An Art Form in Search of its Metaphysics." *The Journal of Aesthetics and Art Criticism,* 42(1):17–27.

Huff, Mac. n.d. *Quartet Coaching Technique Manual.* Kenosha, WI: Society for the Preservation and Encouragement of Barber Shop Quartet Singing in America, Inc.

Kamerman, Jack B., and Rosanne Martorella, Editors. 1983. *Performers and Performances: The Social Organization of Artistic Work.* Contributors: Howard S. Becker, Joseph Bensman, Robert Faulkner, and Stephen Couch. New York, NY: Praeger Publishers.

Kaplan, Max. 1990. *The Arts: A Social Perspective.* Rutherford, NJ: Fairleigh Dickinson University Press.

Lilienfeld, Robert. 1987. "Music and Society in the 20th Century: Georg Lukács, Ernst Bloch, and Theodore Adorno." *International Journal of Politics, Culture and Society* 1(2):310–336.

Maquet, J. 1971. *Introduction to Aesthetic Anthropology.* Reading, Mass.: Addison Wesley.

Mowitt, John. 1987. Pp. 173–197 "The Sound of Music in the Era of Its Electronic Reproducibility." In *Music and Society: The Politics of Composition, Performance and Reception.* Editors Richard Leppert and Susan McClary. Cambridge: Cambridge University Press.

Nutz, Walter, Editor. 1989. *Kunst, Kommunikation, Kultur: Festschrift zum 80. Geburtstag von Alphons Silbermann.* Frankfurt am Main; Bern; New York; Paris: Verlag Peter Lang.

Plasketes, George M. 1989. "Rock on Reel: The Rise and Fall of the Rock Culture in America Reflected in a Decade of Rocumentaries." *Qualitative Sociology* 12(1):55–71.

Rummenhöller, Peter. 1978. *Einführung in die Musiksoziologie.* Wilhelmshaven: Heinrichshofen.

Shepherd, John C. 1983. "Conflict in Patterns of Socialization: The Role of the Classroom Music Teacher." *La Revue Canadienne de Sociologie et d'Anthropologie* 20(1):23–43.

Shepherd, John C. 1979. "Music and Social Control: An Essay on the Sociology of Musical Knowledge." *Catalyst* (Canada) 13(Spring):1–54.

Shepherd, John, Phil Virden, Graham Vulliamy, and Trevor Wishart. 1980. *Whose Music? A Sociology of Musical Languages.* New Brunswick, NJ: Transaction.

Shepherd, John C., and Graham Vulliamy. 1983. "A Comparative Sociology of School Knowledge." *British Journal of Sociology of Education,* 4(1):3–18.

Silbermann, Alphons. 1973. *Empirische Kunstsoziologie. Eine Einführung mit kommentierter Bibliographie.* Stuttgart: F. Enke.

Silbermann, Alphons. 1957. *Wovon lebt die Musik: Die Prinzipien der Musiksoziologie.* Regensburg: Gustav Bosse.

Spayde, Jon. 1990. "Joyful Noise: Can't carry a tune? No Problem. At Singalong, Everybody is a Star." *Continental Profiles* (January):25–50. [Airline Magazine.]

SPEBSQSA. 1974. *Chorus Director's Manual.* Kenosha, WI: Society for the Preservation and Encouragement of Barber Shop Singing in America, Inc.

SPEBSQSA. 1987. *Information Manual for the Barbershop Quartet.* Kenosha, WI: Society for the Preservation and Encouragement of Barber Shop Quartet Singing in America, Inc.

Stebbins, Robert A. 1978. "Classical Music Amateurs: A Definitional Study." *Humboldt Journal of Social Relations* 5(2):78–103.

Stebbins, Robert A. 1978. "Creating High Culture: The American Amateur Classical Musician." *Journal of American Culture* 1(3):616–631.

Stebbins, Robert A. 1976. "Music among Friends: The Social Networks of Amateur Musicians." *Revue Internationale de Sociologie* (Italy) 12(1–2):52–73.

Stroh, Wolfgang Martin. 1975. *Zur Soziologie der elektronischen Musik.* Berg am Inn and Zürich: Amadeus.

Supicic, Ivo. 1987. *Music in Society: A Guide to the Sociology of Music.* Stuyvesant, NY: Pendragon Press.

Wallis, Roger, and Krister Malm. 1984. *Big Sounds from Small Peoples: The Music Industry in Small Countries.* London, England: Constable & Co, Ltd.

Weber, Max. 1917. "Der Sinnder "Wertfreiheit" der soziologischen und ökonomischen Wissenschaften." *Logos, Internationale Zeitschrift für Philosophie der Kultur* VII:40–88. [Extensive discussion of sociology of music.]

Zwellwecker, Ferdinand. 1972. Pp. 27–39. "Einige Überlegungen über die Musik, ihre elektronische Reproduzierbarkeit und Produzierbarkeit." In *Materialien zur Musiksoziologie,* Elfriede Jelinek, Ferdinand Zellwecker, and Wilhelm Zobl. Wien and München: Literaturproduzenten.

SPEBSQSA's Future: Tradition and Innovation

MAX KAPLAN

Major Traditions

The barbershop tradition—indeed, the existence of the organization—rests on two American values. One is universal, shared by all nations: the celebration of its past. The second is more characteristic of us: the celebration of the social group as a fulfillment of individualism.

All societies mark the past, first as a pure narration of their histories. This is inscribed in their written or oral records, and memorialized in holidays, written accounts, documents, legends, and tales of cultural heroes. This may be seen as a vertical approach to the past. A horizontal view of the past consists of celebrations that perpetuate a general mood or quality of the nation taken out as a slice from the narrative. A nostalgia for songs of a certain period falls into this type of tradition. On a larger aesthetic canvas, all nationalistic art falls into this category.

The second, or uniquely American tradition that shaped barbershop is its dependence on the group. Unlike the historical tradition, this is social and psychological in nature. It is not a narrative with dates and events, but a state of mind, an emphasis on social patterns and organization. In the vernacular, this characteristic value in the United States is seen as the "need for approval;" it expands the limitations of individualism; it relies on an ability to organize. Its contribution to barbershop singing is, therefore, the American tradition of joining.

Both nostalgia for something (a selective empathy for the past) and joining with others (a selective association in the present) give rise to all the other elements and purposes of SPEBSQSA; as we will see, they contribute to its purposes and its strengths, and paradoxically, to its risks for future existence.

As to the second, the joining into groups or associations, we can do little better than to turn to Max Lerner's brilliant volume, *America as a Civilization: Culture and Personality*. In a chapter on Character and Society, Lerner writes[1]

> the associative impulse is strong in American life: no other civilization can show as many secret fraternal organizations, businessmen's 'service clubs,' trade and occupational associations, social clubs, garden clubs, women's clubs, church clubs, theater groups, political and reform associations, veteran's groups, ethnic societies, and other clusterings of trivial or substantial importance.
>
> When the intellectuals speak scornfully of Americans as 'joiners,' they usually forget to include themselves; there are more academic organizations in the United States than in the whole of Europe. They have in mind a middle-class American who may be a Shriner or an Elk, a Rotarian, a Legionnaire, a member of a country club . . . In the Warner studies of 'Yankee City' (Newburyport) which had 17,000 people, there were over 800 associations, about 350 of them more or less permanent. . . . At least 100 million Americans were estimated to belong to some kind of national organization.

The motivations among men for joining associations are probably much the same now as they were forty or fifty years ago, when Lerner was writing or when SPEBSQSA was formed: to enjoy the special interests of a given group, to "get ahead" professionally, to "meet people," to confront "loneliness," to get out of the house. Lerner further observes that the American man defines his "social personality" in the "horizontal" connections provided by church, lodge, club or even the political party.

The need "to be needed," an increasing item among the probes of counsellors, is an additional motivation—or experience—that comes to fulfillment in chapters of the barbershoppers. In chorus activity as well as in quartet singing, this interweaving and integration among the members is a fact of barbershopping life. Witness the fact that in the Alexandria Harmonizers, one of the largest and most successful chapters, chorus members are required to attend the final four rehearsals before a contest, and in the final rehearsal several videotape cameras put the actions of every singer into permanent form for evaluation and improvement.

The fact that barbershopping manifests two strong American traditions does not guarantee the permanence of the organization, for even familiar patterns and deep-seated institutions are not immune to social change. Note the passing of the family physician or the music teacher coming to the home of patient or pupil, early architecture (including the town square and band shell), storytelling, the corner saloon, barbershop bowling, the *turnverein*, or newspapers in English, Italian and Spanish—the same paper, as in Ybor City, Florida—the family grocery store, the outdoor political debate, or the one-room school. Yet, amidst dramatic change such as the emergence of the megalopolitan area and culture, there remain such values and action patterns as the love of nature, the family picnic, the county fair, July 4th fireworks, cynicism about the law, suspicion of politicians, amateur and professional baseball, Christmas baskets for the poor, and the Salvation Army.

It is unlikely that either the American nostalgia for the past or the urge for joining into human associations will disappear or weaken, in spite of the advent of change itself as an American value, the ease of mobility in residence, or the growth of faster electronic communications as counter-thrusts to human sociability. On the matter of nostalgia, the actor-producer-keen observer, Woody Allen, has said:[2]

> Who, in the unemployment-based, poverty-threatened, collapse-haunted, revolution-spectored 1930s, only three short decades later and following the greatest period of affluence American society has ever known, would suspect that nostalgia for the 1930s would run rife in the land. And what makes this fact truly fare for the God's laughter is that this nostalgia is as much to be found among American youth—evidenced in popular songs, movies, automobiles, books and heroes from all spheres—as it is among those in their dotage.

In addition to these major traditions, nostalgia and group life, there are secondary or internal traditions with barbershopping that emerge from its unique substance and structure.

Secondary Traditions

I. There has developed among the barbershoppers an almost religious moral quality that is unmistakable to an outside observer. In my extensive 1987 report to the group I spelled out several models or prototypes of organization: the military, business, governmental, religious and family models. My conclusion:[3]

> Accepting some elements of family as a rough model for the barbershop structure, the religious model seems most closely akin to the Society's ethic and sense of morality and preservation of a tradition.

Its body of musical literature, carefully approved by special judges; its chapter symbols and rituals; its "cathedral" in Kenosha; its annual retreats (Harmony College and district sessions); its annual festivals and pilgrimages (competitions); its patron saints (Cash, Hall) and their disciples; the loyalty of its members—these are all religious parallels and elements.

From this complex or "closed system," as some sociologists would call it, there seems to flow a morality, a camaraderie. It comes not only from a unity of objectives and commitments, but from the fact that this brotherhood is built around a process known to all creators in the arts, and especially to performers, i.e., the unity that comes from the rehearsals and production of a piece—the process that moves from a decision to perform the shared learning of the material and its ultimate presentation. All performers go through these steps in greater or lesser detail, length, depth, or struggle—whether as soloists or in groups, instrumentalists or vocalists, amateurs or artists, in chamber ensembles or in the masses within orchestras, choruses or opera companies. Ask a group of raw amateurs who have just gone through some six weeks of nightly theater rehearsals to describe what has taken place in human as well as aesthetic terms. They might (as in groups to which I belonged in my younger years) recall unplanned love affairs and intense quarrels, but also the common pride in the collective accomplishment. And such is the pride that may emerge among barbershoppers that the moral overtone goes beyond friendship into a fellowship of such power that it may keep the member in the fold for several decades.

II. Service to community is the second internal tradition. Performance by barbershoppers might have been limited to ceremonies, concerts, or shows, as in the case of school groups, church choirs or community choruses. However, SPEBSQSA chapters have moved beyond these legitimate, but limited purposes. They have taken upon themselves a practice of contributing their time and talents to a wide variety of community agencies, helping, for instance, to raise large sums of money annually. In this regard, the international association is committed to the Institute for Logopedics in Wichita with the catch phrase "We sing that they shall speak."

III. Another facet of the tradition—perhaps more pertinent to folk rather than to fine art—is *motion*, or physical freedom in expression through song. It is, of course, possible to stand quietly while performing, and there are songs where emotion would be ill-suited, even offensive; the sense of the words determines appropriateness in this matter. Some choruses, numbering over 100 men, may execute patterns that are far more intricate and subtle than anything done by a band on a football field. A psychological factor, not consciously formulated but implicit for middle-class America, is the opportunity given to men who are normally hesitant in expressing their emotions, and who for the most part—as I observed when playing with a dance band—are poor dancers.

IV. There is an internal, structural tradition within SPEBSQSA that is significant in affecting the future: the unusual practice of having all of its officers and musical staff come from the membership. This sets the familiar analysis of Max Weber about bureaucracy on its head,[4] for there is no gap in communications between officers or administrators and the membership. Among American businesses as a whole, officials are professional persons, perhaps trained for the job of management in schools of business. One is not aware that officers of Coca Cola were chemists or bottlers, or that Iacocca spent an apprenticeship on Detroit's assembly lines. Since the point will be made later that the organization, as well as the musical tradition and practices will affect the future of barbershopping, significance of this tradition becomes evident.

V Finally in my view, the most important of the secondary traditions for SPEBSQSA is the emergence of two, three, and soon, even four traditions of singers within many of the families. In this fact we have one of the major clues to the ongoing strength of the organization as well as a significant clue to the very nature of the commitment made by members to barbershop singing.

With computerized record-keeping, SPEBSQSA is now in a position to develop careful records of "generations" as a basis for longitudinal studies in future years by succeeding social scientists. While SPEBSQSA officials are wont to deplore the loss in total membership in recent years, I would submit that a more important statistic is in the growth of two- and three-generational memberships, now that the organization has attained its half century. A rough schemata might take as its hypothesis that members who in 1940 were twenty years old would have had a twenty-year old son by 1960, who in turn would have a son of twenty years in 1980; and if all were alive in 1980, we may assume a grandfather who is only seventy, with a great-grandson of ten. The age of seventy is no more unusual. Even allowing (1) that there will be the birth of girls well as boys, (2) that some members will have had no children, and (3) that not all sons, or sons of sons, will be interested in this activity, we still have a demographic dynamic that opens the prospect of three and four generations in barbershopping. Certainly, the hypothesis hardly needs proof that the presence of fathers and sons in any leisure organization is a strong, positive statement that augers well for the future.

To provide some basis for longitudinal studies along these lines, I prepared a statement for the March, 1989 issue of *The Harmonizer*, inviting families of two or three generational members to identify themselves by letter. In the next several months, replies were received as follows:

- *Twenty-four pairs* (father-son), or forty-eight individuals, responded from Ontario, New York, South Carolina, Kansas, Maryland, Washington State, Nebraska, Oklahoma, Mississippi, New Jersey, California, Illinois, Minnesota and Massachusetts.
- *Five sets* of three-generational members responded from Iowa, Kansas, Massachusetts and Illinois.
- *Three sets* of four-generational members responded from Minnesota, Washington, and one state that was not identified.

Among these responses were cases where family members had spread out geographically, where special efforts are being made (as in family reunions) to be together occasionally with barbershop singing as a major incentive. In several cases, wives responded in lengthy letters to testify positively to the impact of this activity on family life. Several letters spoke of sons who are still too young to be members but who sing with fathers or older brothers and are headed toward membership. One letter by a black man noted the legacy of singing these songs from his father, who in those days was not a member. The impact of generational members can be construed from several quotations.

An Idaho member has four sons, "all who have considerable musical abilities and love singing barbershop." One son, twenty-six, is a school music director, and as a member of SPEBSQSA, sings in both a chorus and quartet. The writer of the letter and his second son, twenty-four, are starting a new chapter in a neighboring community. The third son, twenty-two, sings in a choral group of the university he is attending. The fourth son, nineteen, has been a chapter member in the past, and is now with a university choir. Even the wife fills in as tenor when needed. The father ends, "There is a standing joke (yet somewhat serious) around our home that I audition all girls that my sons are dating to make sure that music will continue in our family. . . ."

The wife of another member writes,

> We have two sons, the eldest of which spent much of the first six years of his life around barbershoppers (I think the first song he learned was not a nursery rhyme, but "Down Our Way") and we have no objection at all if they discovered and continued the pleasurable tradition of barbershop singing in a third generation . . . we have always found barbershopping to be a great family hobby.

These, then, are two primary and five secondary traditions that contribute to the strength of barbershopping. The last of the secondary group will, in time, become as powerful as the basic commitment to preserving the songs they enjoy or the American need for joining. A recognition of these traditional values inclines the outside observer to see the organization from a perspective somewhat different than that which is familiar to the singers. Theirs is a more internal or immediate view of enjoying the literature in its "style" that is guarded by the decisions of trained judges. From a perspective of the next half century, aesthetic or traditional guidelines may prove more flexible than the social heritage we have noted above.

Innovations

It is impossible to evaluate the power of these traditions for the future of barbershopping, without at the same time noting the potentials for innovations or changes; the final task is an attempt to balance tradition *vis a vis* innovation within the larger historical and social factors that go far beyond the limited patterns of leisure. Traditions may be affected by both internal and external developments. The first may emanate from experiments within chapters, from demographic composition of chapters, or from internal schisms. Those based on outside social conditions might be new work/leisure patterns, changing musical and entertainment tastes, or new values in the society as a whole. Obviously, clear lines between internal and external cannot be drawn.

INTERNAL INNOVATIONS: EXPERIMENTS

Experiments by barbershop chapters have been few. There is little incentive to do so musically, given the general acceptance of the literature and style of performance. A critical control over these traditions is the judging system accepted by quartets and choruses. The singing of non-certified arrangements is done, but not in the competitive framework.

Experiments or deviations will more likely appear in organizational aspects, based on local conditions, personalities, and geographical traditions; even in organizational matters there are guidelines issued by the Kenosha staff, such as manuals to help each officeholder; there are training sessions for leaders in the COTS program, including skills in community relationships—all referred to as "chapter craft."

One interesting experiment was in the Bryn Mawr Chapter of Philadelphia. Discussions took place among members to define their philosophy and vision. The result was a decision to broaden the choice of commitment—chorus singing, quartets, or a variety of related activities while rehearsals took place, such as training in vocal techniques. Other "break out" activities included sight singing for beginners, video presentations, or rehearsal by small groups. Fourteen months later the membership had risen from 116 to 143, the chorus added a third performance to its schedule, registered quartets expanded from three to eleven, and nine men attended Harmony College in August rather than the usual three.

Other innovative attempts might be drawn, as in the scenarios below:

1. Experiments that take the time of chapter meetings to turn attention to the origins of SPEBSQSA through a study of the U.S. at the time that the movement began formally, indeed, to earlier periods when such singing took place informally. Strategies could be built around tapes, written records, lectures, discussions, perhaps with guidance from nearby history departments and the Library of Congress or the Society for Popular Culture.
2. Experiments that seek to develop relationships with other institutions in the community or region, such as those concerned with leisure patterns, musical activities, welfare units, hospitals, counselling programs, drug rehabilitation centers, and the like. Our assumption is that barbershoppers have techniques and a philosophy of potential use of other persons and groups, not on basis of treating illnesses but of the contemporary "wellness" movement.
3. Experiments that develop musical alliances with female barbershoppers. Relationships of men and women have changed markedly in recent decades. Attempts to develop

professional relationship can cover a variety of purposes, resulting now from the respective and respected strengths of each.

INNOVATIONS: DEMOGRAPHIC COMPOSITION

A changing population structure may be considered as an "external" source of innovation imposed upon the organization we are examining; indeed, this may have a profound impact. Those men who were in their twenties at the time of SPEBSQSA's founding (1938) and who are alive and still active are now in their seventies. Some are members with records of over forty years of activity. Obviously, the bulk of members now in their forties and fifties came into the group some decades after its birth, during the years of membership expansion and the maturation of both chapter and competitive activity.

It is worth noting that as these post-pioneer members entered the ranks in the 1950s, 1960s and 1970s, dramatic changes were taking shape in the United States and Canada, in leisure patterns generally and in entertainment particularly. Those decades saw a steady growth in the ownership among 98% of homes of one TV set, and 60% with two or more. Other changes were taking place in family patterns, in transportation, in education (especially the growth of adult education), and (as Etzkorn notes elsewhere in this volume) in the use of "loudspeaker" rather than "live" music. The past decade alone has seen changes multiply in the home, especially—notes Trish Hall in the *New York Times* of March 29, 1990—"a revolution in the relationship between Americans and home electronics." Much standard equipment in the home of today was "virtually unavailable ten years ago." Since 1980, for instance, while expenditures on furniture did not change in that decade, with actual lessening for clothing, shoes, food, or gasoline, personal expenditures for electronics went up 45 percent. It is relevant to the fortunes of barbershopping, as well as all leisure or recreational interest, to inquire into the perceptions and values related to material changes, but even more important into new anxieties, new concepts of success, implications of the women's liberation movement, population moves to America's Sun Belt, the recognition by men of a "mid-life" crisis and that many changes in careers are normal, even desirable patterns.

Perhaps our expectations became lowered in recent decades, with growing doubts about professions and offices that had traditionally been honored, whether businessmen, lawyers, physicians or politicians. The future itself came to be questioned, raising doubts about our industrial prowess or even of technology itself. Familiar household and community patterns, among them the perpetuation of familiar songs, became anchors, accepted as a social and personal "good."

INTERNAL INNOVATIONS: SCHISMS

Innovations may result also from schisms among members of barbershop chapters. Our study suggests that there are differences that arouse considerable arguments, even the withdrawal of members. From an outsider's view, these are generally of a minor order, on such matters as the minimum size of chapters, the points to be given for this or that action on the stage, or which choruses should be eliminated or chosen on the basis of regional representation. When the Future II Committee issued an extensive report, most of it dealt with the internal how-to-do matters, using the term "future" in a limited temporal sense.

More serious differences have arisen between members who are critical of the attention paid to choruses in light of the original purpose to encourage and preserve quartets, even though about 80% of all members express a primary interest in chorus participation. Most vocal in the criticism of chorus activity—or emphasis—is a publication that issued its first exchange of letters in September 1987, in an informal publication directed to members for a small subscription fee. Calling itself GUBOS (Give Us Back Our Society), ten issues appeared before 1990.* Led by a strong-minded editor, most contributions stress the "straying" from the original path set forth by the founders, charging that some chapters expel members for failing to attend a prescribed number of chorus rehearsals; that the merging of chapters takes place to produce larger choruses. A GUBOS Manifesto of June 1988, based, says the editor, on collective suggestions, includes the conclusions that "No one has ever learned to be a quartet man by being in a chorus;" that choruses take away meeting time; and that the function of SPEBSQSA is not to "progress" to a high art form, but to preserve. On the other hand, the editor concedes (March 1988) that "people in Kenosha have been doing a fine job and have been pushing for more quartetting. Unfortunately, their efforts will always fall short without pressure at the chapter levels. . . ."

---

*See the essay by Max Brandt in this volume.

In the same set of exchanges, representatives of the SPEBSQSA administration hold that good choral program teaches men how to sing and gain self-esteem so that they can sing in a quartet (Executive Director, March 1989). Another response calls attention to the presence already of subsidiary groups (SIGS, special interest groups) such as the Pioneers who gather annually to "woodshed." He notes that the current chorus champions (Alexandria Harmonizers) are in the same chapter that has won awards of its number of quartets. In a direct call to check into the matter currently, I was informed on December 5, 1989 that aside from its nineteen registered quartets, that very night's meeting would judge some twenty-five "put-together" quartets.

Our view is that such debate is healthy, preventing rather than nurturing serious divisions in the Society. GUBOS provides an outlet for divergent views on a scale not possible in the international journal *The Harmonizer*.

Again, to the outsider, the most direct challenge to SPEBSQSA would occur if it was to develop a sizable and coordinated membership which wanted to forego competitions altogether, whether for quartets or choruses, and to move toward "festivals." The public school system has been able to go in both directions, but even in their competitions among performing school orchestras, bands and choral groups, evaluations are not attempted to the decimal point but on more general judgments of "good," "excellent," "superior." More than one group may emerge with the same rating—a fact generally overlooked by the proud local paper. An example of comment along this line is this excerpt from a letter that appeared in the *Florida State Music Educator's Journal* for Fall 1989, by Dr. A. Byron Smith.

> As the president of the 2600-member Florida Music Educators Association, which includes music educators from kindergarten through college in all areas of music (elementary, band, choral, orchestral, and college music education), I would encourage the use of the word festival rather than competition. We music educators believe that these events are evaluation festivals ... with a national standard for their size of school, performing group and the years they have been together. The dictionary definition of competition is a 'vying together with others for profit, prize or position or a contest of skill.' The connotation of competition is contrary to our desire to evaluate our groups with the intent to improve their performance, keeping all of our educational values in mind.

An even more direct challenge that could develop into a serious schism, even the withdrawal of chapters, would be on the issue of limitations to the traditional literature. Seemingly without major dissent, the organization's imprimatur has already been put on songs that have been composed in recent years, including some by members of the organization itself. Thus the time frame has already been violated: Cole Porter and Irving Berlin tunes are apparently adaptable to the barbershop style, alongside those by Stephen Foster. No quartet or chorus has yet insisted on having an out of bounds song in a competition, and meeting resistance, gone to the courts. This would approximate the legal action of Pete Rose, accused of gambling in sports, seeking a judgment in the Ohio courts rather than following the procedures of organized baseball. An even more serious schism might arise, this time with the court probably accepting the case, if a chapter invited female members or sought to bring a female conductor—and there are some—to the competitive stage.

That none of these schisms has developed with serious threat is perhaps due largely to the structure described above, in which officers and administrators are also members. Further, the dedication to the central "vision" or purpose is presently strong enough to ward off such potentials for internal troubles.

As in many organizations where there is a strong ideology, schisms are more likely to develop from differences in personalities and leadership styles. In such cases, issues will be exaggerated or created to sharpen personal differences or images. Among the more honest differences that will cross between the internal and the external factors will be the presence in the same organization of men who may differ as much as fifty years in age. The aging of the membership, at least until about A.D. 2030, will favor both more purism or nostalgia and more chorus activity. By then the elderly, now about one-tenth of the national population, will be up to one-fifth, a ratio that may well be paralleled in this organization.

EXTERNAL INNOVATIONS

Far greater problems confront us as we consider the future of the barbershoppers in relation to a range of changes in our Society and the world as a whole. Such events as wars and inventions affect us all personally or in our groups and institutions such as family, community, or nation. There is no need to summarize the enormity of these changes in daily life, work, education or recreation since the time that this organization was born before World War II. In the course of that half century, many other groups have failed, many patterns of life and leisure have folded; why has barbershopping been kept alive?

Now, as we begin the last decade of the century, these changes continue. In a popular summary of "What's Ahead," the December 25, 1989 issue of the *US News and World Report* notes a few measures of change: by A.D. 2000, 80% of women between twenty-five and fifty-four will work (70% today); one-third of all families will be childless, with one or more grandparents moving in; about a third of the population (27% now) will have a college education, and the typical college degree will cost $100,000; while we now have 54,000 persons over 100 years old, there will be 108,000; workers will change jobs ten times in a lifetime, and change careers three times; now, two in ten households have personal computers, and this will go up to seven. What will such changes imply, or lead to?

In social science, attempts to explore causality offer immense difficulty. Perhaps no one has gone beyond the successes of a sociologist of another era, William Ogburn of the University of Chicago.[5] His exploration of the telephone, for instance, has not been surpassed as he traced its many paths of impact. Who could today set definite parameters on the influence of television or the computer? Further, it is clear that the more specific the target or recipient—such as a particular leisure activity—the more difficult and involved is the attribution of causes and consequences.

It is patently unwise to predict just which social or technological innovations will have, might have, could have, direct or indirect influences on the future of SPEBSQSA. Even hindsight in such matters may be suspect.

There is, however, another approach that is more tractable: to project a major trend in general rather than to isolate one or more particular stimuli. Of the many that might have impact on our subject group, I select two: one is entirely national, uniquely characteristic of the United States, the second, a recent international series of political revolutions.

The national trend is an inevitable consequence of an increasingly complex, "Third Wave" Society,[6] especially within a capitalistic setting that for many years felt it was threatened by another superpower. Further, following a surge of Federal expenditures for social welfare programs, such as Social Security and expansion of governmental services, a strong administration took over in the 1980s whose ideology was to curtail services while building military defense; an enormous national deficit resulted. The consequence was, and will continue to be in the foreseeable future, cuts in public health, in aid to education, and especially, in funding to assist state and municipal services. The so-called "peace dividend," a possible reallocation from the expected decline in defense, is not probable.

One inevitable result has been the pressure on public agencies to search for methods of integrations, combinations, interrelationships or "networks." Many corporations, for instance, now support a variety of public causes by releasing selected employees during work days, weeks, even months.

The barbershoppers have assisted many public causes by performing for them, by helping to celebrate local holidays, even by an ongoing multimillion-dollar fund to help support a speech research program and clinic. Networking is more directly attained in its youth program, in which the singing style and literature is brought to high schools. This understandable and laudable program is a way of introducing a new generation to its traditions, and suggests a growing respect by the school systems. Yet even this is not genuine networking; it is one-sided.

To qualify for activity within an interweaving process, SPEBSQSA's experience, skills, and enthusiasm need to give and to receive, to participate actively with such skills or concerns as education (especially among adults), therapy, family counselling, the anti-drug program and environmentalism. After fifty years, SPEBSQSA has accumulated an enormous experience in management organization, recruitment, publishing, teaching, training judges and chapter officials. Thus far these skills have been hoarded, almost as a collective secret. Its songs have, indeed, been making public statements on human values, for example, affirmations on the importance of love and friendship, and even on social issues, as in the hilarious satire of the medical profession by the quartet known as "Chordiac-Arrest." Were such able groups to turn their attention also to drugs and environmentalism, they could—intentionally or not—have social impact.

On a purely musical level if, indeed, the barbershop "style" of singing and arranging produces a vocal sound that is both distinct and grand, these techniques have not made a dent upon that segment of music teachers, mostly on the university level, who teach harmony or choral techniques. Again, if there exists within the 800 chapters a significant level of "bonding," clues could be made available to community centers, to the recreation and therapy professions, even to psychiatrists and the "wellness" movement. It is not a one-sided responsibility, for such agencies or professions should be searching for ideas and skills. Such a widening influence would contribute to the permanence of SPEBSQSA.

A second, comparatively macrocosmic impact on SPEBSQSA is conceivable from the international scene. It is a historical coincidence that just about the time that the barbershop tradition in song is spreading to other parts of the world, political/economic revolutions are surfacing on the eastern European front, with the replacement or the transformation of Communist regimes. Further, on the western European front, starting in 1992, there is the introduction of the European Economic Community; and on the Asiatic front (our "Pacific rim"), a burst of economic activity and potential political upheavals, once initiated but now suppressed in China.

A major consequence of these movements will be an increase in openness between cultures; *glasnost* in the USSR has already provided evidence of possibilities. Meanwhile, on a comparatively microcosmic level, affiliated groups of barbershoppers are now found in twenty-eight countries, on the continents of Africa, Australia, Europe and Asia. To plan and coordinate this expansion there is now a World Council within SPEBSQSA. I have advocated the importance of a philosophy as well as a policy, and in that direction, have met with the Swedish cultural officer in Washington, to explore possible liaisons between the cultural institutions of both countries.

It is difficult at this early stage to anticipate what meaning this growth outside of the American continent may have for the future of the organization or the activity. It may well be the most significant factor in the second half century of SPEBSQSA, contributing to a pride among its membership as well as some small influence in shaping person-to-person cultural attitudes. It is probable that foreign groups, especially in the Eastern, African or Asiatic areas, cannot take for granted a knowledge that Americans already have about the Society that gave rise to this literature. They will want such historical and interpretive analysis, and SPEBSQSA will be called upon to provide it in one form or another.

Here an interesting paradox becomes possible, suggesting a danger for the future of SPEBSQSA in the assumption of nationalist traditions per se, as well as danger from the international trend.

As to the first, nostalgia toward American traditions may be challenged by the current and rising historical illiteracy of American youth. While I cannot go all the way with Alan Bloom's critique of American education, there is little doubt of its factual basis.[7] E. D. Hirsch verifies this with his data in the volume *Cultural Literacy*.[8] The present elderly generation of SPEBSQSA members all saw the 1930s or earlier; they grew up in the time of the Model T and Charlie Chaplin, radios, horse-drawn fire engines, corner saloons, mom and pop grocery stores, physicians who came to the house, street gangs who went so far as to steal candy on Saturdays from the neighborhood store, immigrant homes with little English to be heard, and family pride in the child who graduated from high school.

Their grandchildren, even those who have grown up in barbershop homes, take for granted their high-powered cars, satellite TV receivers, drugs among their peers, high-priced college careers and all the other "essentials" of a complex life. All are at home in computer centers with displays of software that my generation of elderly often finds bewildering.

Among this younger generation, Bloom may be right: a loss of contact with values of the past. If this accounts, in time, for a fallout among the potential third and fourth generation in barbershop families, the blame may be largely due to SPEBSQSA's lack of policy toward its past, i.e., a failure to place its cultural heroes and its literature into a wider social perspective.

Eastern Europeans who come to sing this literature in the style of its American origins are historically conscious; they are informed about their own origins. This is also the case in the western cultural areas; while German youth are well acquainted with our "wild west" tradition, their grounding is unfortunately based on the writings of a popular writer who had never been to the United States, and adopted a movie-oriented approach to his subject.

SPEBSQSA's 100th anniversary, in A.D. 2038, will most likely be celebrated within the patterns of our nation and the world at that time—patterns that are not to be anticipated with assurance. The barbershoppers, however, maintain their present traditions or structural formulae, and will make a small contribution toward the cultural continuities over the decades. Indeed, it is precisely in periods of profound change that the cultural historian searches for factors of stability as well as innovation. His special task is to interpret for others the dynamics of balance or imbalance between the two. As I write, the reunification of the two Germanies is a major world issue, and among the questions being asked is—in view of two great wars of our century and the Holocaust—have these people "changed" from the evidences and tragedies of their past nationalism?

But "continuity" and "discontinuity" are terms that for the scholar demand more specific measures, guidelines or "social indicators," than come from editorial writers or columnists. The very nature of flexibility between these two poles becomes a technical and interpretative skill. The contribution by Robert Stebbins in this volume implies that even as a relatively stable element or influence in American society, SPEBSQSA will more likely survive if it serves the functions of an "artistic safety valve," permitting more experimentation to free new members from "a significant degree of monopoly control over the production of their music...."

The analysis of this essay suggests that the experimental or innovative tendencies toward expanding the "style" are being felt, and to some degree expressed now, and not too timidly. There should result no serious threat to the major traditions that have been recounted above, notably the factors of nostalgia and sociability; the first leans on history, the second on human needs. Social modifications usually flow from stage A to stage B, then C, not in the dramatic sequence of 1989 Europe, A to O. SPEBSQSA, a microcosmic component in the present and changing world, hardly suggests a scenario of A to O, even of A to C in a quick pulse of time; there is no apparent need, as there was in the dramatic economic failures of Eastern national entities. Despite some loss in membership among the male barbershop organization, the three organizations committed to this style and content are thriving, respected, and widely known. They share a powerful momentum. They all project and represent a significant value of song within the context of social and human values.

Rather than a flat prediction on the future of SPEBSQSA on a time frame of its second fifty years, the following recommendations are summations of my observations of the past three years as its consultant; these will also summarize the analysis of the present paper. Continuity may well exist without regard to these recommendations; but my view is that these implementations will help assure SPEBSQSA's survival.

1. More attention, especially in recruitment, should be paid to men of middle age and older, including those planning for retirement, approaching retirement, or already retired.
2. Major attention should be given to families which presently or potentially include three, even four generations of barbershoppers.
3. Within limits of privacy and dignity of the individual, the personal, professional and educational histories and skills

of members should be computerized for potential availability to legitimate purposes of the international organization.
4. Within the present program of orientation and chapter dynamics, more attention should be given to the historical, social and aesthetic origins of barbershopping.
5. More experiments are recommended by chapters, districts, or the organization as a whole, in respect to structure, literature, public presentation, adaptability to personal needs, methods of judging, and institutionalization of the festival format.
6. More flexibility is urged in regard to limitations and freedoms within the competition tradition with respect to principles of democracy and gradualism.
7. The confidence and skills demonstrated by barbershoppers within their private (read: almost secret) environment need to be made available to non-barbershop musical and social circles, within established practices of community exchange and networking.
8. SPEBSQSA is urged to encourage, plan for, and incorporate social research into its permanent agenda, through research fellowships, grants, permanent staff, or alignments with established and sympathetic agencies or institutions.
9. As the international aspects of barbershopping become increasingly visible, attention is urged to its full implications and possibilities beyond structural relationships or exchanges, extending to musical, social, even political levels, and preferably in cooperation with ministries of culture or other relevant institutions in each nation.
10. Finally, as an organization that is consciously and systematically tied to traditions of past cultural history, its ultimate values and criteria of success will best be served by eschewing such contemporary foibles as image-making with Madison Avenue techniques, and accepting the fact that by now the barbershoppers are widely known, well-respected, serving a significant function in the continuity of our collective culture, affecting thousands of men and their families—and act accordingly with justified pride and self-confidence.

Notes

1. Max Lerner, *America as a Civilization*, vol. 2, New York: Simon and Schuseter, 1957, pp. 630–31.

2. Woody Allen, quoted in Robert Nisbit, "On Futurology," in *The Third Century: America as a Post Industrial Society*.

3. M. Kaplan, *The Barbershop Society: A Many-Splendored Thing*. Kenosha: SPEBSQSA, 1987.

4. Max Weber, Bureaucracy, in *From Max Weber: Essays in Sociology*. H. H. Gerth and C. Wright, editors. New York: Oxford University Press, 1946, pp. 196–264.

5. William F. Ogburn, *Social Change*, New York: The Viking Press, 1927.

6. Alvin Toffler, *The Third Wave*. New York: William Morrow, 1980.

7. E. D. Hirsch, *Cultural Literacy*. New York: Houghton-Mifflin, 1987.

8. Allan Bloom, *The Closing of the American Mind*. New York: Simon and Schuster, 1987.

Contributors

PHILLIP BOSSERMAN: Ph.D., sociology and social ethics, Boston University and the University of Paris, 1963. Professorships: Boston University, Dartmouth College, University of South Florida, Salisbury State University (currently head of sociology). Survey of educational system in Liberia, 1968–69; study of French sociology, 1981–82 (NEH Fellowship). Books on French sociology and leisure in modern society; numerous papers in international journals. Past president of the International Sociological Association. Research Committee on the sociology of leisure. Several books in preparation including one with J. Dumazedier, University of Paris, on the characteristics of postindustrial society in Europe and the United States.

MAX. H. BRANDT: B.S. (University of Southern Maine) in Music Education, M.A. (University of California, Los Angeles), and Ph.D. (The Queen's College of Belfast - North Ireland) in Ethnomusicology. Peace Corps Volunteer (Nigeria) 1963–65 which included research in West African music. Taught music in grades K–12, Seattle Public Schools, 1970–73. Research Associate at the Inter-American Institute of Ethnomusicology and Folklore, Caracas, Venezuela (Estudio Etnomusicologico de Tres Conjuntos de Tambores Afro-Venezolanos de Barlovento - Caracas 1987) and various places dealing with ethnomusicology. Presently director of Academic Affairs for Semester at Sea, University of Pittsburgh, and Adjunct Faculty in Music Department, regularly teaching Music on Latin America and Introduction to World Music. An avid woodshedder since the 1940s, twelve-year member of SPEBSQSA, member of Ancient and Harmonious Society of Woodshedders (AH-SOW), and has attended both the Baltimore and Chicago woodshedding sessions in recent years.

K. PETER ETZKORN: Ph.D., Princeton University, 1959. Professorships: University of California-Santa Barbara; American University of Beirut; University of Nevada. Currently, chairman of the Department of Sociology, University of Missouri-St. Louis. Visiting professorships: Florida, West Germany, Austria. Review panels, National Science Foundation and HEW. Editor, publication series, Society for Ethnomusicology. Founding member, Inter-American Organization of Higher Education. Editor, Studies in Sociology of Culture, Art and Music, JAI Press. Author, three books and numerous papers here and abroad. International lecturer. Editor, *Music and Society, The Later Writings of Paul Honigsheim*.

J. TERRY GATES: Doctorate: University of Illinois, arts education foundations, 1974. Advanced studies in conducting with Thor Johnson and double bass with Radivoj Lah. Faculty positions: Northern Illinois University, University of Illinois, Muskingum College, Ohio State University, University of Alabama; currently, director of Music Education, SUNY at Buffalo. Organizer and Director, The Alabama Project: Music, Society and Education in America, involving over forty prominent music education authorities. General editor, *Applications of Research in Music Education*, and editor, *Music Education in the United States: Contemporary Issues* (University of Alabama Press, 1988).

MAX KAPLAN: B.E., University of Wisconsin-Milwaukee, 1933; M.Mus., University of Colorado, 1941; M.A. University of Illinois, 1948 and Ph.D., 1951, major in sociology, minor in anthropology and political science. Professorships: University of Illinois, music and sociology; Boston University (director, arts center), Bennett College (academic dean); University of South Florida (director, Leisure Studies program). Author, twenty-five volumes in areas of leisure, arts in society, gerontology. Consultant assignments included: Japanese business and governmental groups, Iran (Cultural affairs and plans for Farabi University), Canadian Arts Council, Israel, Puerto Rico, Lincoln Center for the Performing Arts. Former president, leisure research commission, International Sociological Association. As violinist, many solo concerts, concertmaster of several symphony orchestras, New Southern Trio, member faculty quartets.

DEAN ATLEE SNYDER: A.B., 1925 and LL.D., 1946, Baldwin-Wallace College. Graduate studies in sociology and political science, Columbia University; legal study at Ohio State university and the University of Michigan. Varied career as school administrator, Chautauqua superintendent, senior status administrator for the Civilian Conservation Corps and other agencies under the New

Deal; deputy director, Office of Community War Services, WWII; post-war status as senior officer in the Office of the Secretary, U.S. Department of Health, Education and Welfare, retired in 1973. Hobby participation as a quartet singer since 1922, member of SPEBSQSA since 1945 as international officer and historian; author of many articles for the Society's magazine, the *Harmonizer;* presently, Historian Emeritus.

Bibliography

Considering the ramifications of barbershopping—historically, aesthetically, educationally, psychologically, sociologically—there has been a surprising paucity of serious studies of the movement as a whole or of the male and two female organizations.

In the course of our present studies, three Masters dissertations were found. All are presently in the Heritage Hall Museum of Barbershop Harmony, Harmony Hall, 6315 3rd Avenue, Kenosha, Wisconsin, 53140–5199, Ruth Blazina-Joyce, Curator.

McDonnel, Carol. "An Ethnographic Study of Male Singing." Department of Anthropology, State University of New York—Buffalo Hobby Group, 1980.

De Wolfe, Elizabeth (née Ferringo). "The Group Experience in Barbershop Performance." Department of Anthropology, State University of New York—Albany, 1985.

McKenzie, Edward. "Volunteers in Harmony: a Study of Satisfaction in a Barbershop Chapter." School of Business and Management, Pepperdine University, 1980.

Monica Riedler, an opera soprano in Vienna, wrote an extensive paper, "Barbershop: Musikalische und soziale Aspekte eines kulturellen Phänomens im angelsachsischen Raum," for the Hochscule für Musik und darstellende Kunst, Abteilung Musikpädagogik, 1992. (It is on file in Kenosha.) Her home: Kumpf G. 5/19 A-1010 Wien, Austria 0222/513 70 94.

Several scholars whose essays appear in this volume have prepared additional papers, expanding their interest in barbershoppers. These include:

Etzkorn, K. Peter. "New Media as Instruments for Preserving the Past and Building a Future through Education?" Seminar Educational and Media Practices and Policies as Agents in Shaping Cultural Identity, July, 1992, Chiba, Japan.

Etzkorn, K. Peter. "Mediamorphosis: A Challenge to Traditional Music Education." Seminar, Music Education and the Changing Media Landscape, July/August, 1990, Vienna.

Stebbins, Robert A. "Hobbies as Marginal Leisure: The Case of Barbershop Singers." *Loisir et Société/ Society and Leisure,* 14, 1991.

Stebbins, Robert A. "Costs and Rewards in Barbershop Singing." American Sociological Association, Cincinnati, August, 1991.

Bibliography

During his period as consultant to the Future II Committee of SPEBSQSA, 1987–90, the editor prepared several reports for the organization and for publication:

Barbershop Harmony Society: A Many Spendored Thing, 130 pp. a study directed to the organization, published by it, 1987.

An Ideal Leisure Case Study: the Barbershoppers, *Leisure Information Quarterly*, New York University, 15.1, 1988.

Pages 71–73, in *The Arts, a Social Perspective*, Fairleigh Dickinson University Press, 1990.

50-page summary of Barbershop Harmony: a Many-Splendored Thing, in *Essays on Leisure: Human and Policy Issues*, Fairleigh Dickinson University Press, 1991.

The Harmonizer is the official publication of the Society for the Preservation and Encouragement of Barber Shop Quartet Singing in America. It is published in January, March, May, July, September and November at 7930 Sheridan Road, Kenosha, Wisconsin, 53140. Subscription to non-members is $12 yearly, or $2 per issue.